Has satan Pulled Another One on You?

by

a Friend of Medjugorje

MAJOR BEST SELLERS BY A FRIEND OF MEDJUGORJE

Words From Heaven—Messages of Our Lady from Medjugorje
(50 PRINTINGS)
How to Change Your Husband
I See Far
Look What Happened While You Were Sleeping
It Ain't Gonna Happen
They Fired The First Shot 2012
Medjugorje Prepare the Way for My Final Coming
Fasting
Whose Opinion is Right? And The Painful Truth
Big Q, Little Q
The Nine Days Before Christmas
The Corona Vision
The Plan for Nonbelievers From Dark to Light and the Resistance Against it
The David Answer
Blind to Your Wrong
Medjugorje and the Mysteries of Saint Joseph

A Friend of Medjugorje has written over 800 short books and has produced and hosted over one thousand broadcasts. Several of his books have gone over the million mark.

For additional copies, contact your local bookstore or call Caritas of Birmingham at 205-672-2000 USA.
Or go to mej.com and click on Shop Online

Published with permission from SJP Lic. COB.

ISBN: 978-1-878909-51-0

Printed and bound in the United States of America.

Table of Contents

iii FOREWORD

vii EMPIRICALLY PROVEN

1 INTRODUCTION

CHAPTER ONE

5 satan DECEIVES YOU IN MANY WAYS

CHAPTER TWO

13 PSA—PAY SPECIAL ATTENTION

CHAPTER THREE

29 WE HAVE FALLEN UNDER his SPELL

CHAPTER FOUR

45 THE LOSS OF SOVEREIGNTY IS TAKING PLACE OVER CHILDREN

CHAPTER FIVE

55 "DUMBED DOWN" BY THE SYSTEM

CHAPTER SIX

63 NOTHING ELSE IS REQUIRED. PRAY AND FAST.

CHAPTER SEVEN

91 IT'S ALL ABOUT MONEY—LOTS OF IT

CHAPTER EIGHT

95 satan IS IN THE DETAILS: TO LINK SHOOTING TO PSYCHIATRIC DRUGS, FOLLOW THE MONEY

CHAPTER NINE

113 WHAT REALLY IS A.D.D.? YOU WILL GET THE ANSWER.

CHAPTER TEN

133 KIDS ARE RAISED LIKE VEAL

CHAPTER ELEVEN

151 CATTLE HANDLING FACILITIES

CHAPTER TWELVE

189 HEALING NATURE'S WAY

CHAPTER THIRTEEN

233 A REMEDY FOR OUR WOUNDED AND RESTLESS HEARTS

CONCLUSION—PART I

253 DO NOT REMAIN PARALYZED
MAKE WAR

CONCLUSION—PART II

299 ARE YOU GOING TO STAY IN EGYPT OR START HEADING TOWARDS THE PROMISED LAND?

317 PICTORIAL SECTION

363 ENDNOTES

368 INDEX

381 ABOUT THE WITNESS

Foreword

THE VILLAGE SEES THE LIGHT is the title of a story which "Reader's Digest" published in February 1986. It was the first major news on a mass public scale that told of the Virgin Mary visiting the tiny village of Medjugorje, Bosnia-Hercegovina. At that time this village was populated by 400 families. Over the years, hundreds of major media outlets across the world have continuously given coverage of these events, including *ABC News Program 20/20*, *Life Magazine,* television investigative program, *Unsolved Mysteries*, *The Lasting Sign*, a documentary hosted by Martin Sheen, just to name a few.

It was June 24, 1981, the Feast of John the Baptist, the proclaimer of the coming Messiah. In the evening, around 5:00 p.m., the Virgin Mary appeared to two young people, Mirjana* and Ivanka*. Around 6:40 p.m. the same day, Mirjana and Ivanka, along with four more young people, Milka*, the little sister of Marija, Ivan, Vicka*, and Ivan saw the Virgin Mary. The next day, June 25, 1981, along with Mirjana, Ivanka, Vicka and Ivan, Marija* and Jakov also saw the Virgin Mary, bringing the total to six visionaries. Milka* and Ivan only saw Our Lady once, on that first day. These six have become known as and remain "the visionaries." To date, August 2022, the apparitions continue daily.

Many who will read this book have been following the writings of a Friend of Medjugorje for over 36 years. His original and unique insights into the important events of our day have won credence in millions of hearts around the world. His moral courage in the face of so many leaders caving into the pressures of a politically correct world is not only refreshing, but backed by tens of thousands of written testimonies, has helped to

* The names of the six visionaries at the time the apparitions began: Mirjana Dragičević, Ivanka Ivanković, Marija Pavlović, Vicka Ivanković, Ivan Dragičević and Jakov Čolo. As all of the women have sinced married, their last names have changed.to Mirjana Soldo, Ivanka Elez, Marija Lunetti and Vicka Mijatovic.

deeply strengthen those who desire to live Christianity in its fullness. His insights, that are often proven prophetic, have their source in the apparitions of the Virgin Mary in Medjugorje. Deeply and personally influenced by a Biblical worldview and the events surrounding Medjugorje, he gave himself to the prayerful study and application into his life of the words that the Virgin Mary has been speaking over four decades. He discovered that She has come to speak to mankind in this time because the dangers we face are on a scale unlike any the world has ever known. Millions have been deeply affected by his writings.

—Caritas of Birmingham

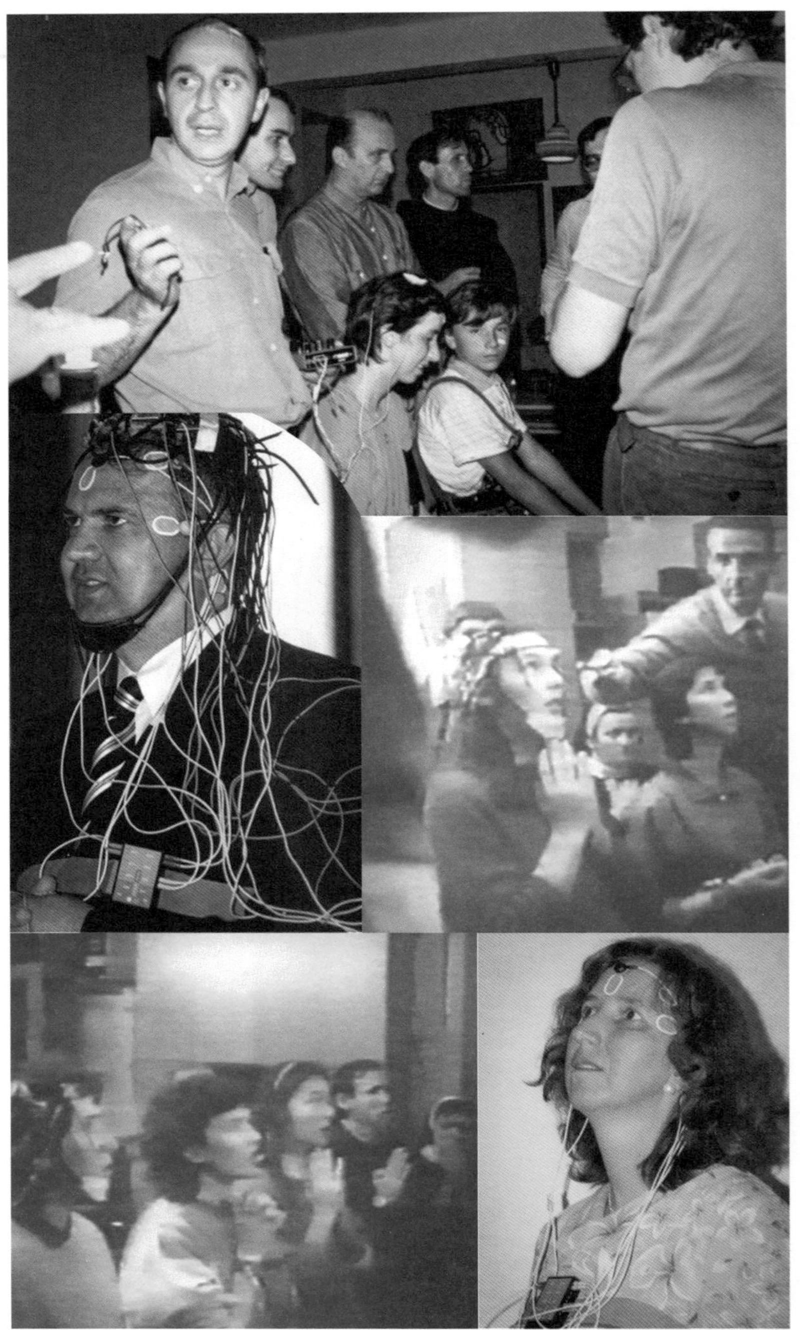

Empirically Proven

What you are about to read is rooted in the apparitions of the Virgin Mary in Medjugorje. Before you reject what is presented in this book, read the following proof that what is happening is real.

FIRST: The Medjugorje apparitions are proven authentic without doubt by empirical evidence; approved through empirical scientific methods. What is empirical evidence? Empirical evidence is the information obtained through observation and documentation of certain behavior and patterns or through an experiment. Empirical evidence is a quintessential* part of the scientific method of research that is applicable in many disciplines. In the scientific method, the pieces of empirical evidence are used to **validate** or **disprove** a stated hypothesis, statement, or claim. In the scientific world, a hypothesis can be accepted by the community by the evidence. If the empirical evidence validates what

* Representing the most perfect or typical example of a quality.

is studied, all of the community can accept its truths. On the other hand, if empirical evidence fails, disproving what is tested and studied, the community can accept the disproving evidence.

While reading this book, one is free to ignore the happenings of the phenomenon of Medjugorje, but in doing so, one would be choosing to ignore the 22 years of scientific testing that took place from 1983 to 2005 conducted by over 20 scientists and doctors. The comprehensive studies utilized the most modern means of testing available from the scientific world. That along with the collected empirical evidence gives infallibility to the conclusion that **the "community of believers" can accept that the apparitions are valid.** While science cannot affirm that it is the Virgin Mary appearing, the final statement and verdict of the scientists and doctors both scientifically and empirically affirm that the six visionaries are:

"ABSENT OF DECEIT."

In other words, teams of scientists have determined that these apparitions are of supernatural origin. Twenty-three years of testing, evaluation, and the proof of changed lives are a testament to the reality that God is speaking to the world today in the village of Medjugorje through the Virgin Mary. What will manifest from the reality from these apparitions is Biblical. The Virgin Mary is the "Woman of Revelation." Revelation 12:1 states:

> ***"A great sign appeared in heaven: a woman clothed with the sun, with the moon under her feet, and on her head a crown of twelve stars."***

The six Medjugorje visionaries **see exactly** what is described in the Bible. Our Lady of Medjugorje **is** the Woman of Revelation. The Bible verses of Revelation tells us what She is here to do. **She is here to crush the serpent's head.** Tragically, the Church has not always embraced what is scientific and empirical, yet, at the top of the Church they embrace things like the Climate Change agenda, that empirical and scientific research has disproved. Just as the Church rejected and condemned astronomer, Galileo, and his research until 350 years later Pope John Paul II declared that he had been right, so too will the Church be humbled in refusing to take seriously the scientific research of the six Medjugorje visionaries and embrace the seriousness of Our Lady's visitations and Her messages of which She has given 415 message on the 25th of each month starting on January 25, 1987 to July 25, 2022. The messages are for the healing of the world..

There are going to be those who will be wailing and lamenting because they not only didn't believe and accept empirical proof, but they ignored or rejected God's answer to heal mankind and the Church. How will they know that they have failed to accept the greatest spiritual event since Jesus' time on earth? Our Lady has given 10 Secrets*, three of the Secrets will be released. Ten days before the First Secret is to be released a priest will

* Visit Mej.com to read in-depth about the 10 Secrets.

be given the First Secret of the three by Medjugorje visionary, Mirjana. Three days before the admonition to the world happens, the priest will announce it to the world. After a short time for conversion, the second secret will be announced three days before it happens, just as the first. The third secret will come the same way. The six visionaries have said the third secret will be announced the same way. The visionaries have relayed that the third secret will be a supernatural sign that will appear on the spot of the first apparition on Apparition Mountain in Medjugorje. It will last until the end of time. It will be indestructible. No armament will be able to destroy it. It will call the whole world to conversion and to return back to the Heavenly Father, and the Virgin Mary's Son, the Christ.

Despair and lamentation will fall like rain across the entire world when the Secrets begin, especially so within the Church. Men will strike their chests when they finally realize after 40+ years what has passed them by. Our Lady said:

August 25, 1997

> **"...now you do not comprehend this grace, but soon a time will come when you will lament for these messages..."**

With Gratitude and Love,

Friend of Medjugorje

Friend of Medjugorje

July 13, 2022, AD

—NOTE FROM THE PUBLISHER—

For those who approach this writing with skepticism concerning the apparitions of the Virgin Mary, whether you are of a faith that is inclined to reject such apparitions or a nonbeliever, we suggest that you not let that dissuade you from reading this book, but simply read the messages of the Virgin Mary as comments such as a pastor would make. <u>Has satan Pulled Another One on You?</u> places in the hands of the reader the answer to the crisis of truth that faces youth and the family today. Deep prayer to the Holy Spirit is necessary to grasp what it is God wishes to tell you through what you are about to read.

YOU WILL NOTICE THAT satan's NAME IS NOT CAPITALIZED

satan does not deserve respect or honor when references are made to him. For years, a Friend of

Medjugorje has not capitalized satan's name or any reference to him, because we refuse to give him this honor or recognition. Why should the application of grammar rules apply to him who has an insatiable desire to be exalted, even above God? We refrain in our references and writings from giving him the same stature afforded even a dog's name. We are not radical in that we don't tell others they must do the same. It is up to each individual to decide for themselves. For the harm satan has done to man, whom he despises, we will not grant him what is even reserved for a dog, the capitalization of his name.

—Caritas of Birmingham

Introduction

Where was satan hiding in the Parkland, Florida, school shooting on February 14, 2018? Is everything to be blamed on anger, hatred, mental disease, sickness or other explanations? You will be surprised to learn that money plays a large part in tragedies such as the Marjory Stoneman Douglas High School shooting in Parkland, Florida! Money is the real evil.

1 Timothy 6:10

> ***"For the desire of money is the root of 'all' evils..."***

The Virgin Mary said on November 2, 2016, **"...expose evil..."** A Friend of Medjugorje has a long history of exposing evil, even when doing so is unpopular and, even dangerous. It is one thing to be a sinner, as Peter told Jesus in the boat, after Jesus calmed the raging sea, *"Depart from me Lord,* *for I am a sinner.*" We must admit we all are sinners. But what makes up the foundation of today's evil is a denial of sin. Exposing those who think what they do is not a sin or who simply don't care, is unpopular and dangerous. When you finish this book, you will be upset, you will be angry, even furious, along with other emotions. It is justified. Jesus rose up in righteous anger, turning the money changers' tables over and whipped them out of the temple. It is time to do the same to the schools, as well as to those complicit in propagating a crime, as you will discern as you read. Do not enter into reading this book until you have first entered into prayer.

"The devil wants nothing more than to crush you. he wants to steal from you everything you value. he wants to kill everything in your life that's good. Ultimately, he wants to destroy you. ***If he can claim the victory over your mind, he can eventually claim the victory over your life."***[1]

Louie Giglio

Don't Give the Enemy a Seat at Your Table: Taking Control of Your Thoughts and Fears in the Middle of the Battle

CHAPTER ONE

satan Deceives You in Many Ways

Truth passes through three phases:

1. It is ridiculed.
2. It is persecuted.
3. It is accepted.

In our age, the Spirit of God is so lacking in the heart of man that he has no discerning wisdom, and so, falsehood reigns. Falsehood goes through three phases:

1. It is accepted.
2. It is challenged.
3. It causes confusion.

Our Lady* says:

* The Virgin Mary is referred to as Our Lady as a term of endearment.

September 25, 1990

"...satan is strong and wants to destroy and deceive you in many ways..."

Many ways? What is Our Lady speaking of? The deception satan makes use of is often right in front of us, part of our society, part of our lives. You might be surprised how you are participating in plans of falsehood. Often satan influences your thinking, leading you to believe that you are doing the right thing. he can even disguise himself in your acting out of love and care. When Our Lady said, **"...(satan) deceive(s) you in many ways...,"** do not think it is only in the obvious circumstances of what would be sinful. satan is very clever in disguising his plans in order to guide the masses towards ruination. But, neither think "the masses" excludes you. We are a part of it. In my book, Look What Happened While You Were Sleeping, published in 2007, it shows how to gain a new mentality and how to change your life's situations. Many are doing so.

But the lessons the book teaches must be actively remembered, in order to continue to identify, and then reject the *'many ways' of falsehood satan deceives us through* in order to destroy the culture.

What if we could look into hell and listen in on satan talking to his legions? What if we could have heard about one of his plans before he activated it, a plan that many of you are now participating in and/or have accepted and tolerated in others? A plan satan initiated to be one of the "many ways" that is aiding his master plan to destroy the culture. A plan to deceive and destroy you, which is presently taking place in many of your families. Let's listen in on satan's instructions in hell before this plan was initiated.

> **satan:** *Come, gather around, all of you filled with delightful hatred. i have formulated a plan which i will now initiate upon the earth. Oh, how we will easily invade the youth with this one. If, and curse my lips for saying so,*

the despised Maker of Creation has programmed that the most active participation of parents in the lives of their offspring is during their youth and adolescence, then we must, in turn, be most active in participating in that same period of their lives. you, my dear slime workers of evil, know well that if we capture their ways in their youth, they, in turn, are stuck with struggling the rest of their lives. we must so imprint them with erred thinking and ways for life so they can only escape our happy way of sin and evil with great difficulty.

How will we enslave them? We will persuade a large portion of youth to use drugs to affect a greater portion of youth in bringing more down. Give them amphetamines, drug them out. Make them mundane. Take the most ambitious, those with the most energy and dull them into falling in line with everyone else.

Then, we can condition and brainwash the masses into believing whatever other plans we initiate.

First, we must inspire with pride and greed a great many in my godless academic educational institutions. we will do this through the ignorance and intimidation of the youth's mentors and those who guide them, utilizing also, man's natural selfishness, laziness and pride. Make them prey upon the youth to convenience themselves. Remember, get the drugs into their hands by the schemes i will unfold. Make their normal behavior become abnormal through the use of drugs. Particularly, make the use of amphetamines plentiful, and with great speed, but with stealth deception, spur them on to addictions. Use our delectable vice of selfishness to move the influencers of the youth to convenience themselves so, through the deception of helping the youth, we demons can sell the idea to youth to take drugs. We will manufacture disorders so that we can change the normal youth to help the worm called "man" create a new world without God through the valuable trait of greed and arrogance. Now be off and do not forget...deceive, disguise and drug.

You have now listened in on hell's plans. While you are not deceived because you are already aware that there is widespread use of drugs by the youth and you know the harm it causes them, can you be sure that you are not deceived in other ways? The plans of satan are much more clever than you think. Plans initiated, through the temptations of demons, are carried out by man and, therefore, are often difficult to attribute to the devil. They give the appearance of human ideas or plans and, therefore, are not seen as evil. However, read on and see how stealthily satan's plans, about which you have just read, have manifested closer to you than what you think. This particular plan of satan unfolds throughout the next chapters.

"We're making great progress, but we're headed in the wrong direction."[2]

Ogden Nash
American Poet

CHAPTER TWO

PSA—Pay Special Attention

In 1960, the pharmaceutical industry partnered with psychiatry to create a strategy that certain behavioral or emotional difficulties, for the first time, would be called "brain diseases." Hence, "psychopharmacology,"[3] which today is a very lucrative industry, was born, and a marketing strategy was developed to deceive the public into thinking that behavioral or emotional difficulties were a "brain disease," as a result of the brain supposedly being chemically imbalanced. The public's acceptance of an unfounded disease would then allow the marketing of new drugs under the deception of "medicine," medicine that was now said to be necessary to balance out the effect of a chemical in the body that the brain was supposedly lacking.

In 1960, there was no such thing as a psychiatric "disease," just as today there is no such thing![4] For there to be a bona fide disease, there must be verifiable findings, a physical or a chemical abnormality. In the past and to date, with all our research, studies and technology, **there has not been found a single physical or chemical abnormality in life, or by autopsies, that would give evidence of a chemical disorder which would cause depression, bipolar disorders and other mental illnesses,** according to Fred A. Baughman, M.D., as well as other experts.

Dr. Baughman is a respected adult and child neurologist who has testified before Congress, the European Union, and the Parliament of Western Australia that *"all claims that psychiatric diagnoses are diseases are fraudulent."*[5] If there is no chemical abnormality, there is no disease! Therefore, the marketing strategies, put forth to create an abnormality that is without proof, is satan's idea.

Man's greed grabbed this idea and created a brain malfunction, and then offered a drug that appears to fix the nonexistent abnormality. Man grabbed, from satan, the evil plan to create the sickness, an unreal brain abnormality, and then offered the drug as its cure. An appropriate name for this is"Profit from Sickness." The same entities that create the sickness come up with remedies for the sickness. It places greed-driven man in control to manage the industry and its expansion. "Profit from Sickness" is at the beginning, and at the end, of identifying the problem and giving the solution. Now that the groundwork is set, satan, step-by-step, implements his scheme, and evil can go to the next phase.

In 1980, arrogant man, in a committee, invented a new disease without any proof of brain malfunction. The public accepted this disease and still does today, without any proof of its existence 40 years later. They named the invented disease **A**ttention **D**eficit **D**isorder known as **ADD**.[6] Our

Lady would begin appearing in Medjugorje shortly afterwards. Immediately, Our Lady began relaying in the first months of the apparitions that man is suffering from a crisis of faith, that faith was extinguishing itself. Man, by 1981, had put his trust and faith in man, while satan's goal was to help man create a world without God. Confirming satan's plan, through man, Our Lady said:

January 25, 1997

> **"…I invite you to reflect about your future. You are creating a new world without God, only with your own strength…"**

Around the time period of the invention of ADD, through a committee, a pharmceutical company, by the name of Ciba-Geigy Corporation, funded a nonprofit organization called CHADD, which is an abbreviation for **C**hildren and **A**dults with **A**ttention **D**eficit/**H**yperactivity **D**isorder.

(Ciba-Geigy Corp. is now two companies: Novartis and Ciba Specialty Chemicals). CHADD's purpose was to create and increase the market for the drug company Ciba-Geigy. To make it clear: Ciba-Geigy (now Novartis) makes the drug "Ritalin,"* which becomes the answer for the nonprofit organization, CHADD, who in turn hails the virtues of Ritalin as the solution to ADD/ADHD. Would you say that CHADD, being funded by Ciba-Geigy (now Novartis), is a diabolical plan?[7] Shocking? Yes! This is beyond criminal. Millions and millions of youth have damaged, even destroyed, lives because of this criminal liaison. To repeat what was just stated for greater emphasis, Ciba-Geigy (now Novartis) is a pharmaceutical company. Ciba-Geigy created CHADD to legitimize and promote their drug, Ritalin. The public is made to believe that these two entities are separate and independent from each

* Ritalin was first developed around 1948 by CIBA. It was used for a few years very sparingly until around 1955 when it basically went dormant for about 25 years. It wasn't until 1980, when ADD/ADHD was first invented that suddenly Ritalin was activated once again as the wonder drug for ADD/ADHD.

other. This is much more than a conflict of interest; it is an evil agenda, propagated against innocent people, especially the youth, to make them become dependent on drugs—prescription drugs, that have to be filled over and over again. It is like creating your own oil well that will never run dry. All for the love of money. As you continue to read, you will learn of many more crimes that will be just as earth-shattering.

In 1987, ADD was revised [8] and became ADHD. The "H" added to ADD would stand for "Hyperactivity." ADD is the same, but adding the "H" for hyperactivity would apparently gain further widespread use of drugging youth for simply being energetic. Henceforth, in this writing, when ADHD comes up, it includes within it ADD, because, essentially, it is the same thing. What the new medicine or "the cure" does is it sedates people, particularly the youth, with drugs. Where does it come from, that one who has energy and one who is very active and impulsive is labeled with a negative term, "hyperactive," as if being active is wrong? How could anyone with common sense accept that those behaviors are abnormal, a disease, or a sickness? All because the supposed protectors, the mentors of the youth, their teachers, even some parents, do not want to deal with them. Therefore, give the kids amphetamines, stimulants and the like, and disguise it as medicine.

Ritalin, a methylphenidate, and its cousins (Adderall, Vyvanse, Dexedrine, Strattera, Desoxyn, and Guanfacine) are reported to be the most widely used drugs on the market. Hundreds of millions of dollars that come from selling an astounding 46,000 pounds of the drug in 2002,[9] make it the most profitable drug in use today. So, satan has now the funds for many, who are in key positions, to mask the fraud being perpetuated to deceive the public.

When ADD was revised to ADHD in 1987, in order to have a better and wider market for its *"medicine,"* for the invented ADHD, Our Lady came along a few months later, helping us to uncover deceptions, such as giving children "dope" and calling it medicine. Her messages, given in wisdom, address different things, and at different times, as well as speak to us individually. She answered the ADD falsehood with a counter "term" that recommends Her own medicine to the youth that they need for their problems, which is the opposite of using drugs. Our Lady warns us to **P**ay **S**pecial **A**ttention to what is going on. Her answer to **A**ttention **D**eficit **D**isorder is **PSA**, **P**ay **S**pecial **A**ttention. She also reveals what kind of medicine you need to help you pay attention. Again, the following message was given only a few months after ADD was revised to ADHD, apparently to catch more youth in the net. You are about to read a profound revelation, giving support to everything written in this book! Our Lady said:

September 9, 1988

> **"...your Mother is warning that satan is at work. I would like you to** pay special attention **to 'the fact' that satan is at work in a special way 'with the young'...I would like you to talk with your children. I would like you to exchange your experiences and help them to solve all their problems... 'Prayer is medicine' that heals."**

What? Prayer is the medicine! Not according to CHADD, the nonprofit puppet of Ciba-Geigy (now Novartis), the manufacturer of Ritalin, for the created disorder of ADHD. Is this not astounding? Our Lady comes four months after Ciba-Geigy's creation and says, **"...Prayer is the medicine that heals."** And Our Lady, addressing the youth through their parents, when the drugs started spreading a couple of years later, said:

March 25, 1990

"...I want to protect you from everything that satan offers you and through which he wants to destroy you..."

While Our Lady's messages apply to many things, at all times, there remains a historical aspect as well, of when they were given, of what was happening at that moment. You cannot get clearer than these two previous messages, connected with the drugging of the youth, but also to train them, conditioning them to take the easy step, to later become dependant on opioids.*

Many teachers are impatient with youth who require more maintenance, so "doping" the kid is the answer, lest they disrupt the rest of the class of kids who are content to sit eight hours a day. That's the point. Either through laziness or mis'guid'ance, the 'guide' would just as soon label a student as

* Opioids are a class of drugs that include the illegal drug, heroin, synthetic opioids, and pain relievers available legally by prescription and many others.

sick, instead of dealing with them with patience. This truly is misguidance by teachers. On July 15, 1996, Congressman Christopher Shays, from Connecticut, testified in regards to ADHD:

> *"…we are placing millions of children and adults on either side … that divides the healthy from the sick…to make our children medical patients because as a culture we have lost our patience with them…"* [10]

There are behavioral problems in school, but we have been so conditioned to answer them with sedatives, amphetamines and other stimulants, rather than uncovering and correcting the root problem of the behavior. By drugging, we are telling people that the way they behave is not their fault. Few understand, nor do they want to understand, that all we are doing is treating a behavior which is the fruit born of a tree that is the root cause of the bad behavior. It may be caused by a bad family life, drug abuse, bad diet, etc. The child's behavior is not the real problem. The problem is that schools are sedating the behavior, masking the problem, which changes nothing or rather compounds the problems the child is already experiencing. We should, instead, be looking at the root from which some of the more serious behavior is coming from, in order to correct the problem. While we agree that some behaviors need to be dealt with and handled appropriately, a so-called drug free school should be drug free.

No one questions the use of authentic medicine for authentic medical conditions. Behavioral problems are not a medical condition if there has been no proof found of a physical abnormality causing the behavior. Drugging behavior is against Natural Law and, therefore, is immoral. Therefore, treating the behavior with drugs should be illegal. Out of line behavior has proliferated, but this is not due to a brain disease, rather a parent disease, the disease of divorce.

The epidemic of divorce and/or warring and bad parenting in homes is the major contribution to inciting bad behavior and emotional problems in children/youth. Therefore, many disturbances are not a youth problem, but a parent problem. The cure? One part of the cure is the proper exchange of love, authority and obedience between the couple, to each other, and their watchful, diligent forming of a Biblical worldview in their child. This will enable the youth to be all he can be. He will be able to deal with every problem and fulfill God's Will in his life. Yes, it is that simple. Everything self corrects with prayer and a proper environment of love made by the Dad and Mom, especially with each other.

The Ten Commandments must be taught in school, as they give a practice of behavior over man's millions of laws across the land. Can we teach the Ten Commandments in school? Judaism, Christianity, and Islam — all have the same

Ten Commandments. So, who is left to object to the teaching of them? The answer is so few that their voices should not get a hearing, as they too, as nonbelievers, will benefit from a more wholesome society, safer for <u>all</u>. This is the fruit Our Lady seeks—that correct family living brings forth the correct fruit by which society functions.

May 1, 1986

> **"...I wish that the fruits in the family be seen one day..."**

There are other necessary corrections which give solutions for the problems many youth face today. These will be discussed in later chapters, but first we must understand some of these problems in greater depth.

"There are days when I deliberately avoid it (taking Ritalin). You just don't feel yourself. You feel so drained out. It makes you feel disgusted and down. Like you've got no soul or something."[11]

Leon Perry
13 years old

CHAPTER THREE

We have Fallen Under his Spell

It is quite clear that satan, with his hellish plans exposed, created disorders. Greedy man readily accepts the evil inspirations. These do not have to even be authentic disorders. There are certainly phantom disorders concocted, just as the committee did in contriving ADHD, then from Ciba-Geigy's *promotion of ADHD, and its apparently predetermined answer, their drug. The anxiety put upon parents and youth themselves is caused by this phantom disorder that originated in hell; and yet, no one sees it. Anxiety often caused wrong decisions, such as parents letting their child be put on Ritalin, Adderall and other similar stimulant drugs. Our Lady said:

* Ciba-Geigy Corp. is now two companies: Novartis and Ciba Specialty Chemicals.

August 15, 1983

> **"...Do not be in anxiety...Every disorder comes from satan..."**

That includes real and phantom disorders that cause disorder. On April 15, 1998, Dr. Baughman wrote:

> *"The single, biggest health care fraud in U.S. history—the representation of ADHD to be an actual disease, and the drugging of millions of entirely normal American children, as 'treatment,' is spreading like a plague..."*[12]

satan's plans are many, and he is working with every means possible to hamper, damage and destroy millions of lives. Our Lady said:

March 21, 1988

> **"...today again your Mother wants to warn you that satan, by <u>every means possible</u>, wants to ruin everything in you..."**

We fall under the spell. satan's actions are not always obvious, but often as foolish people, we think we are able to track him. It is why Our Lady has come, as She said on September 25, 1986:

> **"...(to) uncover the deception that satan makes use of..."**

satan does not always possess a person to act upon his plans. Many times satan makes use of the sicknesses people have to conceal himself, in order for him to act through the individual under his influence. The following is from The Gospel as Revealed to Me,* in which the life of Jesus Christ is told through Italian mystic, Maria Valtorta. Jesus responds to his apostles and disciples who were speaking about a lunatic who was cured by Jesus earlier. Jesus says:

* The Gospel as Revealed to Me, is a ten-volume set that tells the story of Jesus Christ, from the infancy of the Virgin Mary to the birth of the Early Church. Revealed through Private Revelation to Italian Mystic, Maria Valtorta, in the 1940s, it became widely known when the Medjugorje visionary, Marija, asked Our Lady in an apparition if one could read these books. Our Lady responded by saying, **"One can read them."** Originally, the works were entitled, The Poem of the Man-God.

"I have explained several times to you that every disease, as it is a torment and a disorder, may conceal satan and satan may hide himself in a disease, causing it and making use of it to torture a soul and make it curse God. The boy was ill, he was not possessed. He is a pure soul. That is why I was so pleased to free his soul from the most cunning demon who wanted to dominate it and make it impure."

"Jesus was then asked, 'What is necessary to cast out such demons?'

"Jesus replied:

"'Prayer and fasting. ***Nothing else is required. Pray and fast.****'"*[13]

The plan to take normal youth, invent a disease, call active youth abnormal, feed them regular amphetamines, called "dope" in the 1970s, cannot be regarded in any other way than evil. Dr. Baughman gave a "wow" statement, to the Report on the

Council on Scientific Affairs of the American Medical Association as follows:

> *"Once children are labeled with ADHD, they are no longer treated as normal. Once Ritalin or any psychotropic drug courses through their brain and body, they are, for the first time, physically, neurologically, and biologically, abnormal."*[14]

Do you see, now, how dangerous these false medicines are? Nothing less than poison.

So, what do parents and grandparents do when a teacher says you need to put your loved ones on drugs? The following article that appeared in *Better Homes and Gardens* will give you one of the courses of action to take.

> *"When Sarah Collier's kindergarten teacher suggested she was hyperactive and required medication, her mother, Theresa, fumed inwardly. After taking her own quick time-out*

to cool off, the Rockford, Illinois, stay-at-home mom calmly coached the teacher on how to handle bubbly Sarah.

"Once the girl was seated at the front of the class and given clear directions on what was acceptable in class and what wasn't, she was far less distracted and restless. 'Within weeks, she was just fine and the teacher didn't complain again,' Theresa says.

"That is, until the same teacher had Sarah's younger sister, Haylee, two years later. Once again, Theresa had to steer the conversation away from drugs and toward the same measures that had worked for Sarah. 'After summer break, children sometimes need to settle down and get into classroom rhythm,' she says. 'And teachers need to get used to the new students' temperaments. Kids also have certain ways they learn best.'

"Neither Sarah, now eight, nor Haylee, six, went on Attention Deficit/Hyperactivity Disorder drugs and that has them bucking a national trend. Treatment with Ritalin—the most popular drug used to treat ADHD—and its chemical cousins have skyrocketed.

"'Children with the slightest attention problem are sent to be assessed for ADHD at our clinic,' says William Frankenberger, a psychologist and director of the Human Development Center at the University of Wisconsin Eau Claire. 'We can't believe they were referred.'"[15]

Steven E. Hyman, the director of the National Institute of Mental Health, addressing a conference on ADHD in November 1998, said:

"ADHD affects from 0-3% in some school districts, up to 40% in others. Surely this cannot be right."[16]

It certainly cannot be right, and it reflects that the youth have been betrayed by schools whose mentality is that they do not want to deal with active kids. The mentality of the teachers in schools with high drug use has come from a faculty convincing themselves that 40% of their students need this drug; hence, the "selfishness" and self-interest part of the plan satan devised in hell, preying upon our youth. William B. Carey, addressing the same November 1998 conference, stated:

> *"What is now most often described as ADHD in the United States appears to be a set of normal behavioral variations..."*[17]

And so, there we have it. One of the devil's plans, as he has successfully captured millions of youth, in which they are placed on amphetamines on a continuous basis, often times for years, and it has come through the hands of school officials, who are supposed to be the protectors, advocates and mentors of our youth. Recall that Our Lady said:

September 9, 1988

"...Prayer is the medicine that heals."

One father relayed to us back in the mid-1980s, that he knew without having the facts, but through prayer, to be steadfast in refusing to allow his son to be put on drugs.

"My son was rambunctious, full of energy and more maintenance than his fourth grade teacher wanted to handle. The teacher said he had ADD. Instinctively, as a father, I knew something was very wrong with the picture. I thought, 'Where has ADD been for the last couple thousand years?' Most of the people I knew who were high in energy and had a hard time keeping still ended up coping and excelled in what they did.

"Through the years, the people who addressed and discussed with me what they had determined, repeatedly lost all credibility in my

eyes, because I knew truth in my heart that they were off base. The only problem I observed was that when one had a child with boldness, ambition, lots of energy, etc., these characteristics were being labeled a handicap. 'That' was the problem and the accuser was making it a problem. All the things they were presenting as negative, I had seen as positive attributes, which would help him in life after he learned to manage them.

"Over a 15-year period, these meetings held by the school and others to convince me to put my child on Ritalin did no good. I always sensed that their efforts were not graced by the Light of God's ways. The teachers and an array of other individuals seemed conditioned to give, in advance, always the same pat answer: 'Ritalin him.'

"Throughout my son's educational years, having to go before one pro-ADHD individ-

ual or panel of 'professionals' after another, I did not buy into their remedies. I stood against them, often at the expense of being condemned, accused of not caring or mocked for not knowing what I was doing. Once, I was even ridiculed when in a meeting with a psychologist, a teacher and six sets of other parents. The room was darkened to make it warmer, to lessen the rigidness around a boardroom oval table. One by one, all 11 adults took the bait and fell for the lie, afraid if they went against 'the professionals' they (the parents) would damage their child. All the parents agreed to place their children on Ritalin. It was a very polished setup. The psychologist and teacher had everyone turn on me. I was the lone parent who said an absolute 'no.' I was viewed as a villain and obstructor of justice. I saw through the pressure tactics used in the meeting and the agenda behind it to ostracize anyone who said 'no.' It did not steer me from the truth. The result was that my son had to learn how to control his behavior and, today, he is successful at what he does. Had I not held to my instincts as a father, I do not believe he would have learned methods to compensate that make him excel now in life, nor would he have the talent to do what he is successful at today."[18]

Following is an excerpt from a letter, shared with us by the same father above, to the principal of the Catholic high school his son was attending, after the high school personnel said his son would have to go on Ritalin to stay in their school. The father was explaining why he would not allow his son to be placed on Ritalin.

"I do not want my son to use the label 'attention deficit' as a crutch, and I have never even told him about what I have gone through throughout the years to protect his normal

self. In the long run, I see it would benefit him as an asset and believe strongly, after much prayer, God will help him. He did me, through my schooling, and I overcame it with great difficulty and am better for it. Just like another six year old, who was sent home after his first day in school, with his teacher telling his mom that it was no use in bringing him back because he was too stupid to educate. The six year old went on to do wonderful things. He was Thomas Edison.

"A great many of those whose accomplishments are recorded in history, had these types of problems and once overcome, achieved the near impossible. Many blind people are genius in music. Beethoven was deaf. How many talents and extraordinary skills and discoveries are killed by making so many so-called attention deficit children, 'ordinary' like everyone else, through the use of Ritalin,

when in reality they would have had to overcome failures and great difficulties by cultivating other attributes to a far greater degree, because they supposedly were so lacking in normal achievements. For centuries, men have dealt with what most everyone sees as a problem, but which I see as an asset and allowed by God.

"The saints' lives show us what to do with afflictions/assets, however you view it. Somehow wisdom tells me it is very wrong, at least for my son, if not for others, to fix what teachers and experts say is a problem 'for him' through drugs. For his own perfection, my son needs the problems of struggling through, even if by senior year he barely makes it. Here are just a few people who were told by their schools, just as you have done, that they had so-called 'learning problems' similar to my son's. Their names should speak for them-

selves: Albert Einstein, Abraham Lincoln, St. John Vianney, St. Bernadette, and St. Catherine of Sienna (Doctor of the Church).”

“Lastly, in entering the first grade, I was sent home in the first 10 minutes. Why? Behavior! I bit the daylights out of the teacher because I did not want to go to school.” [19]

The question that should be asked is, would anyone of these people, if they had been born in our time, been able to raise themselves up to be who they became if they had been placed on a behavior-altering drug throughout most of their youth? Wisdom and common sense suggests that the answer is “no.”

"He became a ghost of his former self and drifted around school and through lessons for years...He seemed to have lost the will to live... The only loser in the equation was the pupil, who seemed drugged into stupidity."[20]

*Mr. Tom Bennett,**
Teacher at Raine's Foundation School,
London, England

* A former teacher of Leon Perry, the 13 year old quoted at the beginning of Chapter 3, pg. 28.

CHAPTER FOUR

The Loss of Sovereignty is Taking Place Over Children

Throughout history, behavior was influenced and tamed by Christian and Biblical principles, especially with behavior in need of discipline, whether speaking of self or external discipline. But today, we have replaced discipline with drug use, through man's creative arrogance, kissed by satan. Taming the behavior generally worked, until satan removed prayer from schools, along with the Biblical principles which always served as the medicine needed in the classroom. We took out prayer and, thereby, replaced it with satan. Where there is a spiritual void, it will be filled by satan. Most private schools have also abandoned these principles in lieu of drugs. So, man accepts the alternative plan of restraining certain normal behavior, through making kids drones in the classroom through drugs, instead of letting them develop behavioral methods that would compensate for their energy and impulsiveness, enabling them to manage themselves, tempered by the principles of Christianity. Some may want to present the argument of the pro-ADHD side. There is no reason to give a voice to a false opinion or lend an ear to such. In fact, Our Lady said:

February 14, 1982

> **"...Do not argue. satan exists! He seeks only to destroy..."**

Our Lady teaches us not to argue or debate. You will certainly find arguments debating the other side of the coin of what is printed here (Pro-Ritalin), but **why let the devil give his opinions?** Again, there is no need to debate. A false opinion does not have a right to express its falsehood. When satan kept trying to present his falsehoods to Jesus in the desert, Jesus silenced him, saying, be gone. Listening to a false opinion will only cause confusion. Cutting through the debate is simple. One statement tells all. The marketing that led to the widespread use of Ritalin, in which schools, teachers, school psychologists, etc., were enlisted, was successful because of the nonprofit organization, CHADD. CHADD's funding, as already stated, comes from the company who makes Ritalin, Ciba-Geigy (now Novartis). Case Closed!

However, the **case** may not be completely closed. As stated, falsehood's three phases are:

1. It is accepted.
2. It is challenged.
3. It causes confusion.

The second phase of being "challenged" began through court cases being filed against those who perpetrated this falsehood. Dr. Baughman writes that on May 1, 2000, the law firm of Waters and Kraus of Dallas, Texas, filed the first class action lawsuit, charging that CHADD, among other organizations:

> *"...planned, conspired, and colluded to create, develop, promote and confirm the diagnoses of Attention Deficit Disorder and Attention Deficit Hyperactivity Disorder, in a highly successful effort to increase the market for its product Ritalin."*[21]

By September 2000, five other class action lawsuits had been filed. Baughman continues:

> *"It is impossible to escape the conclusion that ADHD is a total fraud leading to the medical victimization of millions of previously normal...children across the United States."*[22]

However, by the end of 2002, all five of the Ritalin class action lawsuits were dismissed. The first lawsuit to be dismissed, the judge ruled that the plaintiffs *"failed to state a cause of action."* [23] The judge also stated that, *"the allegations were fully without merit. Plaintiffs failed to provide any concrete statements to document their claims."*[24] Obviously, with the dismissal of these lawsuits and the judge's comment, we know there had to be a lot of hanky-panky going on, especially as the evidence has continued to mount over the past 20 years. It is time to reverse the lies.

Many of you do not realize the loss of sovereignty that is taking place over children. It is an unalienable right, built into Natural Law, for parents from God. It does not come from the government or schools or teachers, or other bodies; therefore, they have no authority to diminish or oppress this ordained right. The more these bodies are allowed to do so, to the same degree they will abuse those rights. Do not concede. Rather, exercise your sovereignty over the upbringing of your children, because we live in a time where satan is eroding the Natural Laws of Nature's God, which man cannot interfere with without serious consequences, consequences which lead to the destruction of the family. Parents must be the primary teachers, the primary guides, the primary advisors, and the primary authority over their children. Many are not, because they have conceded too much of the wrong influences over their children. Our Lady said:

October 24, 1988

> **"...your Mother wants to call you to pray for the young of the whole world, for the parents of the whole world so they know how to educate their children and how to lead them in life with good advice. Pray, dear children; the situation of the young is difficult. Help them! Help parents who don't know, who give bad advice!"**

Your children's education is your responsibility. The only thing that has saved our nation, to date, is parents exercising their authority over their children, through options such as homeschooling. Small groups of parents can and should start their own schools. As a parent or grandparent, get your children off drugs. But, in doing so, realize that it may not be as simple as taking your child off the drug, especially if he has been taking it for years. All the time your child has been on the drug, he has not been learning how to cope or compensate for his behavior, or refine areas in which he could excel in.

We know of one story that ended tragically, in which a boy was raised taking Ritalin since he was very young. After he graduated from high school, he took himself off the drug. His family noticed that he was not acting responsibly and would often get into trouble. They began to see that taking Ritalin his whole life left him without any skills to be responsible for himself. He didn't like how the drugs made him feel and didn't want to take them anymore, but, because he was always under the influence of the drug most of his life, he never developed self-discipline. He was never fully in control of himself. Once off the drug, a drug that was simply there to help keep him calmed down, his life sped out of control and he committed suicide before reaching the age of 25. The family believes today that the root problem was that Ritalin hampered this boy's ability to develop into a responsible adult.

More recent research is also revealing that drugs taken over a long period of time, actually stay in the body even after the drug is no longer being taken. Do more research, but realize it is dangerous to stop using an addictive substance abruptly. One must gradually come off the drug, taking lesser and lesser quantities. It could even take up to a year to be fully weaned from it. But, be working towards getting your child (or yourself) off the drug. Replace the drug with prayer and begin to seek positive changes in the life of your child that builds their self-esteem and adds purpose to their life. You will read more about how to do this in the later chapters of this book.

"When they are given Ritalin…it…saps them of their personality and turns them into almost zombie-like children."[25]

S.W.

An Elementary School Teacher

CHAPTER FIVE

"Dumbed Down" by the System

The author of the book, Running on Ritalin, Lawrence H. Diller, wrote to a concerned mother, Sue Parry, who was trying to find research and/or studies which would reveal hard evidence supporting the claim that chemical abnormalities exist in youth who are stigmatized as handicapped because someone, somewhere, said they had, and then labeled them with, ADHD. He wrote:

> *"The reason why you have been unable to obtain any articles or studies presenting clear and confirming evidence of a physical or chemical abnormality associated with ADHD is that there are none."*[26]

Do not go any longer with the lie. St. Paul wrote to the Galatians,*"O stupid Galatians!*[27] *Who has cast a spell over you?*[28]*...After beginning with the Spirit are you now ending with the flesh? How could you be so stupid?"*[29]

People of the spirit can see through the ADHD charade, while people of the flesh have bought into it. St. Paul's witness certainly gives the testimony to call a spade a spade. So it is, therefore, appropriate to say that many teachers are "dumbed down" by the system. How can they be so stupid? They are without thoughtfulness, not challenging something so serious that has conditioned them to recommend drugging kids to make them act differently, without reflection and, therefore, accepting the lie. But many who are reflective and concerned are finally coming to see the truth. The following is one teacher's experience with Ritalin in the schools.

> *"I was a speech-language pathologist in public schools for many years. I attended many*

meetings over these years in which Ritalin was recommended as the solution to the behavioral problems a child was said to be experiencing. I often felt sympathy for parents who would walk into a room full of professionals, including the school psychologist, special education teacher, speech-language teacher, the classroom teacher, other teachers if they had pertinent information to share, the school counselor, and sometimes the principal, or the assistant principal.

"Normally the school psychologist was the one who ran the meeting, and everyone would have their turn to give the results of their testing. The teachers would explain the child's behavior in the classroom. It was a highly intimidating and emotional experience for the parents. All these professionals telling a parent what was wrong with their child based on standardized testing and observations. It can

easily be imagined how small a parent could feel in a situation like this and how hard it would be to stand up against a roomful of teachers who were moving toward a decision to put their child on Ritalin.

"Ritalin was a fairly new drug when I began working in the public schools. As a professional, I suppose I should have questioned this drug and why it was being used so often. But as the new kid on the block, and somewhat naive, I couldn't imagine anyone giving a child something that wasn't good for him. I just didn't question. I think this was often the case for others. I had been trained to think it wasn't my job to know if there was some scheme behind Ritalin. We did what was recommended by the professionals, and it was generally the call of the school psychologist, backed by the teachers' observations.

"Obviously, in light of uncovering the truth about Ritalin, that doesn't hold much water. I certainly saw teachers, and even some parents, who were only too glad to get a child under control to make life easier for them. I knew, even back then, something wasn't right about that, and I had very little respect for those teachers or those parents. There were parents who refused to put their child on Ritalin, and they were generally viewed as uncooperative and stubborn parents within the meeting. The most pitiful cases were with parents who were not well educated themselves, and often poor. They, often, were too overwhelmed by the situation to do more than sit and do what they were told. Just sign here on the dotted line. But there were other teachers, and parents of course, who wanted to do the best for their child and the best, they were told, was Ritalin. And since Ritalin was always put in a posi-

tive light, parents accepted it with confidence. Others accepted it reluctantly, and with many tears. But after all, we all accepted it. The whole nation did. And so we all are responsible for selling out our youth."[30]

Speech-Language Pathologist, Illinois

Once again, who is behind the big push? CHADD. Why? To make money for the company, Ciba-Geigy (now Novartis). How? Through the active participation of evil, through man collaborating with satan. For the one who is in prayer, God will give His wisdom to see. For the one without prayer, it will be difficult.

"…stop drugging our children and youth to control their feelings, thoughts and actions. Antidepressants, stimulants, benzodiazepines and all other brain-disabling, mind-altering drugs should not be used to control the minds or behaviors of young people. Children need more adult help, not more neurotoxic drugs. We must not let them grow up with their brains and minds soaked in neurotoxins…"[31]

Peter R. Breggin, MD
Psychiatrist

CHAPTER SIX

Nothing Else is Required. Pray and Fast.

On Wednesday, February 14, 2018, another horrendous school shooting took place in the United States. The name of Majory Stoneman Douglas High School in Parkland, Florida, will be lodged in the consciousness of our nation for a long time—like Sandy Hook, Columbine, Virginia Tech and others. The

Two mothers weeping after the Parkland, Florida high school shooting on February 14, 2018.

first picture to emerge of the breaking story was of two weeping mothers holding each other—one with a large gray Cross on her forehead. February 14 was not only St. Valentine's Day, but it was also Ash Wednesday—the first day of Lent—and Christians around the world were going to services to have ashes placed upon their forehead. ***"Remember that you are dust, and to dust you shall return."***

As the events played out that day, it became more and more evident that Ash Wednesday wasn't a mere coincidence, but provided the spiritual background to another devastating evil perpetrated upon the youth and families of our nation. It is a spiritual battle that we are waged in, regardless of the secular narrative that dominates the discussions, accusations and news bites each and every time one of these shootings takes place.

Ephesians 6:12

> ***"For our struggle is not against flesh and blood, but against the rulers,***

against the authorities, against the powers of this world's darkness, and against the spiritual forces of evil in the heavenly realms."

satan is active not only in the evil act of killing, not only in the division that these events continue to cause among the people of our nation, not only in the politicizing of these events, taking advantage of the emotional state of so many individuals to move agendas forward in the name of "justice," but also in the way satan hides himself in a crime he has successfully perpetrated in millions of homes, with millions of youth. It is not hidden in the sense that one cannot see the link to his involvement; it is hidden because of the refusal of the media to report this link, and for investigators to dig deeply into the coincidences found in many of the killers. What is the link? Repeatedly, those who have gone on these killing sprees were on mind-altering prescription medications.

Looking at the data of mass shootings in the United States from 1982–2012, of 62 mass shootings that were perpetrated by 64 shooters, 41 of the shooters, 64%, a vast majority, had signs or characteristics for which psychotropic medications would be prescribed.[32] The data since 2012 confirms the same.[33] Now, consider the following list of the most known cases of mass shootings, including school shootings, many of which involve a young person. The drugs highlighted in each of the following cases are linked with many adverse effects. Do not rapidly read through this list, but slowly and thoughtfully read what these drugs potentially cause in the person taking them: mania (behavior marked with periods of great excitement, euphoria, delusions, and over-activity), insomnia, anxiety, agitation, confusion, amnesia, depression, paranoid reaction, psychosis, hostility, delirium, hallucinations, abnormal thinking, depersonalization, lack of emotion, **suicidal ideation**—being preoccupied with suicidal thoughts and ideas, mentally envisioning ending one's life, and **homicidal**

ideation—the mental envisioning and planning of murdering others, often in violent ways. These are only a few of thousands of cases that could be listed here.* Reading the next 16 pages is nauseating and repulsive.

On April 5, 2021, 19-year-old twins, **Farhan and Farbin Towhid**, in Allen, Texas, killed themselves and their entire immediate family, including their parents, sister, and grandmother. They were on antidepressants. They made a suicide pact seeing they were not getting better.[34]

On January 24, 2019, **Zephen Xaver,** age 21, killed 5 people at the SunTrust Bank in Sebring, Florida. Xaver had a history of mental

* The mass shootings in Buffalo, New York (10 killed, 3 injured) and Uvalde, Texas (21 killed) that took place in May 2022, as well as the July 4, 2022, Highland Park shooting in Chicago, (7 killed, 40 injured) are not included here for lack of information. It usually takes months after a shooting before information begins to surface that the shooter was on some type of psychotropic drug, when the story is no longer in the news.

illness*, was a patient in a psychiatric hospital in 2013, and certainly was on psychiatric medication during periods of his life. According to a girlfriend, he was obsessed with death which increased over time. The day before the shooting, he stated to the Washington Post that he wanted to kill people.[35]

On October 28, 2018, **Robert Bowers**, age 46, with a long history of mental illness, opened fire at the Tree of Life Synagogue in Pittsburgh, killing 11 and injuring 6, including 4 police officers. Mental health records were kept confidential.[36]

On September 21, 2018, **Snochia Moseley**, age 26, with a handgun, killed 3, injured 3 others and then killed herself at a Maryland drugstore warehouse. She had been diag-

* When you read "mental illness," this is not always the case. Youth suffer from the way they were raised. When someone is raised in an atmosphere of fighting, arguing, war or are from a broken and divorced family, it is only natural the child will be depressed. If you add to that antidepressants or other mind-altering chemicals, it is like gasoline on a fire. These chemicals affect the brain. There is a blowout. As you read the book, you will be shown the truth of these statements.

nosed with mental illness. and had become increasingly agitated.[37]

On February 14, 2018, **Nikolas Cruz**, age 19, killed 17 and injured 17 more in his shooting spree on Ash Wednesday at Majory Stoneman Douglas High School in Parkland, Florida. According to reports, Cruz and his brother both were labeled ADHD, and took medication as treatment.[38]

On November 5, 2017, **Devin Kelley**, age 26, opened fire during a Sunday morning Church service at the First Baptist Church in Sutherland Springs, Texas, killing 26 and injuring an additional 20. He was on psychotropic drugs since he was a toddler. He was being treated for ADHD and was on high doses of 'psych' meds throughout his school years.[39]

On October 1, 2017, **Stephen Craig Paddock**, age 64, opened fire on a crowd of over 22,000 people attending a Country Music Festival in Las Vegas, Nevada. He killed 59 people and injured over 500 others. He then killed himself. Paddock was on an antianxiety drug, that has a side effect of causing aggressive behavior.[40]

On September 23, 2016, **Arcan Cetin**, age 20, walked into the Cascade Mall in Burlington, Washington, and shot and killed four women. He also shot one man who later died in the hospital from his injuries. He was taking medication for depression and ADHD, including Prozac.[41]

On July 22, 2016, **Ali David Sonboly,** age 18, shot and killed nine people and injuried 27 others at the Munich Olympia Shopping Centre in Germany. He then took his own life. He was taking psychiatric medication at the time of the shooting.[42]

On October 1, 2015, **Chris Harper Mercer**, age 26, at the Umpqua Community College in Roseburg, Oregon, shot and killed eight students and one professor, injuring eight others. After being wounded by police, he shot and killed himself. He was first prescribed medication as a child and continued to take it throughout his life. Whenever he would not take his pills, his mother would place him in a psychiatric hospital. [43]

On June 17, 2015, **Dylann Storm Roof**, age 21, killed nine people during a prayer service in an Episcopal Church in South Carolina. He had a history of taking the mind-altering narcotic Suboxone*, which is used to treat addiction to opioid drugs such as heroin.[44] On a side note, reflecting on Our Lady's words, **"...Do not believe lying voices..."** the media screamed he was a white supremacist,

* Some of the adverse effects of Suboxone include anxiety, irritability, depersonalization, confusion, suicidal thoughts and irrational, sometimes violent behavior.

never referencing that he was drugged. In the February 14, 2018, Florida shooting, the media quickly reported that the shooter, Cruz, was a white supremacist. It was discounted. This is a tactic used many times by the lying media who try to foster division.[45]

On December 15, 2014, **Bradley Stone,** age 35, shot and killed six people in Montgomery County, Pennsylvania, and then took his own life. He was taking the antidepressant Trazodone and the antipsychotic Risperidone at the time of the shooting.[46]

On November 20, 2014, **Myron Deshawn May,** age 31, opened fire in the library at the Florida State University, wounding three. He was taking Wellbutrin and Vyvanse for depression and ADHD. [47]

On June 5, 2014, **Aaron Ybarra,** age 26, went to the Seattle Pacific University and started shooting. He planned to kill as many people as possible, but he was apprehended before he was able to fully carry out his plan. He was successful, however, in killing one person and wounding two others. He was taking Prozac and Risperdal.[48]

On April 2, 2014, **Ivan Lopez**, age 34, opened fire at Ft. Hood, Texas, killing three soldiers and wounding 16 others, before taking his own life. He was taking a **S**elective **S**erotonin **R**euptake **I**nhibitors (SSRI) antidepressant* and Ambien at the time of the shooting.[49]

On October 21, 2013, **Jose Reyes**, age 12, went into Sparks Middle School in Nevada and shot and killed a teacher and wounded two students before taking his own life. He was taking a generic version of Prozac.[50]

* **S**elective **S**erotonin **R**euptake **I**nhibitors are a class of drugs that are typically used as antidepressants in the treatment of major depression, anxiety and other psychological conditions. **S**elective **S**erotonin **R**euptake **I**nhibitors (SSRI) have the governments most serious drug warning attached to them because of the increased risk of suicidal and homicidal thoughts and temptations.

On September 16, 2013, **Aaron Alexis,** age 34, at the Navy Yard in Washington D.C., shot and killed 12 people and injured eight others. He then took his own life. He was taking Trazodone.[51]

On December 14, 2012, **Adam Lanza**, age 20, killed 20 students and six adults at Sandy Hook Elementary School in Newtown, Connecticut. He had been prescribed several psychiatric drugs, including Fanapt*, a controversial antipsychotic medicine. [52]

On September 27, 2012, **Andrew Engeldinger**, age 36, shot and killed seven people, wounded two others, and then took his own life, at Accent Signage Systems, where he was recently fired. He was taking Mirtazapine and Trazodone.[53]

On July 20, 2012, **James Holmes**, age 25, killed 12 people and wounded 58 in a movie

* Fanapt is one of many drugs the FDA pumped out with an ability to exact the opposite desired effect on people...inducing rather than inhibiting psychosis and aggressive behavior.

theater in Aurora, Colorado. Holmes confessed to his psychiatrist a month before the shooting that he was having homicidal thoughts. Found in his apartment were many medications including sedatives and the antianxiety drug, Clonazepam. Also found was the antidepressant Sertraline, the generic version of the antidepressant Zoloft.[54]

On March 8, 2012, **John Shick,** age 30, walked into the Western Psychiatric Institute at the University of Pittsburgh and started shooting. He killed one person and wounded six more. Forty-three different prescriptions were found in his apartment, including antidepressants, sedatives and antianxiety medication.[55]

On October 12, 2011, **Scott DeKraai,** age 41, entered the Salon Meritage hair salon in Seal Beach, California and began shooting. He killed eight people and wounded one more.

He was on an antidepressant and a mood stabilizer. [56]

On April 18, 2009, **Christopher Alan Wood**, age 34, of Middletown, Maryland, shot and killed his wife and their three small children, ages five, four, and two inside their home. Wood's toxicology test showed he had in his system oxycodone, zolpidem, alprazolam, nortriptyline, amitriptyline, bupropion, and acetaminophen. Two are pain relievers, one is for sleeping, one is for anxiety and three are anti-depressants..[57]

On March 29, 2009, **Robert Kenneth Stewart**, age 45, killed eight people and wounded three at the PineLake Rehab Center and Nursing Home in Carthage, North Carolina. He was taking Lexapro, Ambien, and Xanax.[58]

On September 23, 2008, **Matti Saari,** age 22, walked into a high school in Finland and shot and killed a teacher and nine students. He was taking an **S**elective **S**erotonin **R**euptake **I**nhibitors (SSRI) antidepressant*, along with a benzodiazapine, Xanax.[59]

On February 14, 2008, **Steven Kazmierczak**, age 27, walked into Northern Illinois University and started shooting. He killed five people, injured 21 and then killed himself. He was taking Xanax, Ambien and Prozac.[60]

On December 5, 2007, **Robert Hawkins**, age 19, walked into the Westroads Mall in Omaha, Nebraska, and shot and killed eight people and then himself. He had a long history of taking antidepressants, being diagosed with ADHD, mood disorders and depression.[61]

* **S**elective **S**erotonin **R**euptake **I**nhibitors are a class of drugs that are typically used as antidepressants in the treatment of major depression, anxiety and other psychological conditions. **S**elective **S**erotonin **R**euptake **I**nhibitors (SSRI) have the governments most serious drug warning attached to them because of the increased risk of suicidal and homicidal thoughts and temptations.

On November 7, 2007, **Pekka-Eric Auvinen**, age 18, went to the Jokela High School in Tuusala, Finland, and shot and killed eight people, injured 12 and then killed himself. He had been taking an antidepressant for over a year.[62]

On October 14, 2007, **Asa Coon**, age 14, ran through the SuccessTech Academy in Cleveland, Ohio, with a gun. It resulted in one dead and four wounded. He was taking Trazodone a anti-depressant and sedative and Clonodine, a medicine for high blood pressure but sometimes used to treat ADHD.[63]

On April 16, 2007, **Cho Seung-Hui**, age 23, in a killing spree at Virginia Tech in Blacksburg, Virginia, killed 32 people and wounded 17 others. He had prescription psychiatric drugs found among his belongings. [64]

On August 30, 2006, **Alvaro Rafael Castillo**, age 19, shot and killed his father. He then drove to Orange High School in Hillsborough, North Carolina, and shot and wounded two students. He was taking two antidepressant drugs and one antipsychotic drug at the time of the shooting.[65]

On March 21, 2005, **Jeff Weise,** age 16, shot and killed nine people before taking his own life on the Red Lake Indian Reservation in Northwestern Minnesota. He was taking the antidepressant Prozac.[66]

On November 28, 2001, in Franklin, Massachusetts, **Christopher Pittman**, age 12, shot and killed his grandparents. He was taking the antidepressant drugs, Paxil and Zoloft.[67]

On June 8, 2001, **Mamoru Takuma**, a Japanese janitor, age 40, ran through the Osaka Elementary School with a knife and stabbed and killed eight first and second grade children and wounded 16 others. He was taking the antipsychotic Seroquel, the antidepressant Paxil, and the benzodiazepine drug Lormetazepam.[68]

On March 22, 2001, **Jason Hoffman**, age 18, went to the Granite Hills High School in El Cajon, California, and started shooting. He wounded five people. He was taking Celexa and Effexor.[69]

On December 26, 2000, **Michael McDermott**, age 42, went on a shooting spree at Edgewater Technology in Wakefield, Massachusetts. He killed seven people. He had prescriptions for 17 separate medications, including Prozac.[70]

On April 20, 1999, **Eric Harris**, age 18, and **Dylan Klebold**, age 17, murdered 12 students and one teacher and injured another 21 students at Columbine High School in Colorado. Harris was taking Luvox, an antidepressant drug.[71]

On May 21, 1998, **Kip Kinkel**, age 15, murdered his parents and the next day opened fire in Thurston High School in Oregon, killing two students and wounding 22 others. He had been prescribed both Prozac and Ritalin.[72]

On December 1, 1997, **Michael Carneal**, age 14, began shooting students in a prayer meeting at Heath High School in Paducah, Kentucky. He killed two and wounded 22 others. Carneal was on Ritalin.[73]

On October 1, 1997, **Luke Woodham**, age 16, stabbed his mother to death and then drove to Pearl High School in Pearl, Mississippi, where he shot and killed two students and injured six more. He was on Prozac.[74]

On October 12, 1995, **Toby R. Sincino,** age 16, shot and killed one teacher and wounded another teacher, at Blackville-Hilda High School in South Carolina. He was taking Zoloft.[75]

In December 1993, **Stephen Leith**, age 39, walked into Chelsea High School in Michigan and shot and killed the school's superintendent and wounded two others. He was on Prozac.[76]

On September 14, 1989, **Joseph T. Wesbecker**, walked into his former employer, Standard Gravure, in Louisville, Kentucky, and shot 20 workers, killing eight and injuring 12 others. He then killed himself. He was taking Prozac.[77]

On January 17, 1989, **Patrick Purdy**, age 25, opened fire in the Cleveland School schoolyard in Stockton, California. He killed five schoolchildren and injured 32 more. He then took his own life. He had been on Amitriptyline, an antidepressant, as well as the antipsychotic drug Thorazine.[78]

On September 26, 1988, **James Wilson**, age 19, walked into the Oakland Elementary School in

> Greenwood, South Carolina, and started shooting. He killed two eight-year-old students and-wounded nine more. He was taking Xanax.[79]
>
> On May 29, 1988, **Laurie Wasserman Dann**, age 30, walked into the Hubbard Woods Elementary School in Winnetka, Illinois, and started shooting. She killed two and wounded six others. She was taking Anafranil.[80]

By now you might be fighting feelings of hopelessness. But the final solution at the end of this book will set you on the road to stopping this madness.

Many of the medications mentioned in these stories that are given to treat depression, anxiety and other psychotic conditions now come with what the **F**ood and **D**rug **A**dministration (FDA), calls a ***"black box warning"*** – warning that some side effects can cause "suicidal ideation" and even "homicidal ideation," or in other words, suicidal and murderous thoughts. David Kupelian, an investigative reporter who has been studying this trend for many years, writes:

> *"Whether we like to admit it or not, it is undeniable that when certain people living on the edge of sanity take psychiatric medications, those drugs can—and occasionally do—push them over the edge into violent madness. Remember, every single* ***'S'****elective* ***'S'****erotonin* ***'R'****euptake* ***'I'****nhibitors, referred to as 'SSRI,' is an antidepressant sold in the United States of America today. No matter what brand or manufacturer, these homicidal drugs bear* ***a 'black box' FDA warning label****—the government's most serious drug warning—of 'increased risks of suicidal thinking and behavior, known as suicidality, in young adults ages 18–24.' Common sense tells us that where there are suicidal thoughts—especially in a very, very angry person—homicidal thoughts may not be far behind. Indeed, the mass*

shooters we are describing often take their own lives when the police show up, having planned their suicide ahead of time." [81]

Why is there such a lack of curiosity among journalists to dig deeper into this obvious thread that links these mass murders, especially in youth? Kupelian is unapologetic in where he lays the blame:

"Pharmaceutical manufacturers are understandably nervous about publicity connecting their highly lucrative drugs to murderous violence, which may be why we rarely, if ever, hear any confirmation to those first-day reports from grief-stricken relatives who confide to journalists that the perpetrator was taking psychiatric drugs. After all, ***who are by far the biggest sponsors of TV news? Pharmaceutical companies, and they don't want any free publicity of this sort.***

"The truth is, to avoid costly settlements and public relations catastrophes—such as when GlaxoSmithKline was ordered to pay millions of dollars to the family of 60-year-old Donald Schell who murdered his wife, daughter and granddaughter in a fit of rage shortly after starting on Paxil—drug companies' legal teams have quietly and skillfully settled ***hundreds*** *of cases out-of-court, shelling out hundreds of millions of dollars to plaintiffs. Pharmaceutical giant Eli Lilly fought scores of legal claims against Prozac in this way, settling for cash before the complaint could go to court while* ***stipulating that the settlement remain secret—and then claiming it had never lost a Prozac lawsuit."*** [82]

In another example of the complicity of pharmaceutical companies linked to heinous crimes of those who are under the influence of their drugs, Kupelian describes the case of Andrea

Yates, in 2001, who drowned her five children, ages seven years old down to six months old, in a bathtub, while under the influence of the antidepressant drug Effexor. At her 2006 re-trial, Yates' best friend Debbie Holmes testified on her behalf.

> *"Holmes said she helped care for her friend's children in 1999 after Yates returned from a psychiatric hospital following two suicide attempts. Holmes said that a few months later she asked Yates why she had been so depressed. Holmes said, 'She asked me if I thought satan could read her mind and if I believed in demon possession.' Prosecutors cross-examined a neuropsychologist who evaluated Yates about six months after the drownings. Dr. George Ringholz said Yates recounted a hallucination she had after the birth of her first child. Dr. Ringholz said, 'What she described was feeling a presence… satan…telling her to take a knife and stab her*

son Noah.'…Dr. Ringholz said Yates was delusional the day of the drownings and did not know her actions were wrong, even though she called 911 and knew she would be arrested. Her delusion was that satan had entered her and that she had to be executed in order to kill satan, he said. Dr. Ringholz said, 'Delusions cannot be willed away.'" [83]

Yates had been taking the antidepressant Effexor. In November 2005, more than four years after Yates drowned her children, **the FDA required Effexor manufacturer, Wyeth Pharmaceuticals, to quietly add 'homicidal ideation' to the drug's list of 'RARE adverse events.'**[84]

RARE???

SEVEN Thousand Stories is not Rare!

How many more tens of thousands of people are under the spell of the drug effects?

Recently, (January 2022), when doing the final research to complete this book, The source "SSRI stories," was found.* "S*SRI Stories is a collection of over **7,000 real life tragedies,** most of which were published in newspapers or scientific journals. In these reports, prescription antidepressant medications are mentioned. Common to all of them is the possibility—sometimes the near certainty—that the drugs caused or were a contributing factor to some negative outcome."*[85] Research for yourself and find the overwhelming evidence of the evil agenda that is killing our children at a rate that continues to grow more and more out of control.

* The website in which the 7,000 stories involving SSRI, **S**elective **S**erotonin **R**euptake **I**nhibitor, is **https://ssristories.org/**

"Calling for more spending on mental health and on psychiatry will make matters worse, probably causing many more shootings than it prevents."[86]

Peter R. Breggin, MD
Psychiatrist

CHAPTER SEVEN

It's All About Money—Lots of It

Pharmaceutical companies also deliberately down-play the effects of some of their drugs, by stating that the adverse affects only happen in a small percentage of the population. As quoted in the previous chapter, Wyeth Pharmaceuticals states the "adverse events" are "rare." This is misleading or more accurately stated, an outright lie, as Kupelian explains:

> *"The FDA defines it as occurring in less than one in 1,000 people. But since that same year 19.2 million prescriptions for Effexor were filled in the U.S., statistically that means thou-sands of Americans might experience 'homi-cidal ideation'—murderous thoughts—as a*

> *result of taking just this one brand of antidepressant drug. Effexor is Wyeth's best-selling drug, by the way, which in one recent year brought in over* ***$3 billion in sales****, accounting for almost a fifth of the company's annual revenues."* [87]

Solvay Pharmaceuticals, the manufacturer of the drug, Luvox, used by Eric Harris, the shooter of the Columbine High School April 1999 slaughter admitted that:

> *"Four percent of children and youth taking Luvox—that's one in 25—developed mania during short-term controlled clinical trials. Mania is a psychosis which can produce bizarre, grandiose, highly elaborated destructive plans, including mass murder. Interestingly, in a recent controlled clinical trial, Prozac produced mania in the same age group at a rate of 6%. These are very high rates for drug-induced mania-much higher than those*

produced in adults. Yet the risk will be even higher during long-term clinical use where medical supervision, as in the case of Harris, is much more lax than in controlled clinical trials. These drugs also produce irritability, aggression or hostility, alienation, agitation, and loss of empathy." [88]

Contemplate—Luvox causes 1 in 25 children to develop grandiose, highly elaborated destructive 'plans,' including mass murder. **1 in 25!** Prozac is even much higher in developing the same behaviors and even higher in long-term use!

'C'itizens **'C'**ommission on **'H'**uman **'R'**ights, or **'CCHR'** International, also known as *"The Mental Health Watchdog,"* put together the following "fact" points that show the overwhelming evidence that psychiatric drugs cause violence. [89] The data in the following chapter does not include statistics past the year 2012. The numbers have greatly increased over the past ten years.

"The drugging of children in America and increasingly throughout the world is a tragedy. Millions upon millions of children and youth will never know their full potential because they grew up with an intoxicated brain — their neurotransmitters forever deformed by being bathed in these drugs during their formative years. Additional millions will become career consumers of psychiatric drugs with a vastly reduced quality of life and shortened lives. It is time to say, 'No more of this!' and to directly confront the need for stopping this inhumane, destructive approach to our children and youth."[90]

Peter R. Breggin, M.D.
Psychiatrist

CHAPTER EIGHT

satan is in the Details: To Link Shooting to Psychiatric Drugs, Follow the Money

satan hides; he has hidden himself, deceiving masses of people to accept clever disinformation and explanations for these tragedies.

FACT: Despite 27 international drug regulatory warnings on psychiatric drugs citing effects of mania, hostility, violence and even homicidal ideation (murderous thoughts), and dozens of high profile shootings/killings tied to psychiatric drug use, there has yet to be a federal investigation on the link between psychiatric drugs and acts of senseless violence.[91]

FACT: At least 37 school shootings and/or school-related acts of violence have been committed by those taking or withdrawing from psychiatric drugs, resulting in 175 wounded and 82 killed (as of the year 2012).[92] It is difficult to find statistics past 2012, because in other school shootings, information about their drug use was never made public—neither confirming or refuting if they were under the influence, and law enforcement is not required to investigate the use of prescription drugs in criminal acts. From what is gleaned from news reports of individual cases, it is without a doubt that the statistics would be much higher of school shooters under the influence of prescription psychotic drugs.

FACT: School shootings are not the only mass killings tied to psychiatric drug use. There are 63 other acts of senseless violence committed by individuals taking or withdrawing from psychiatric drugs, resulting in an additional 427 dead and 754 wounded (as of the year 2012). [93] Again, the numbers are much higher than what is shown here, but as information is not being made readily available, there is no way to estimate the numbers. The above figures do not include more recent mass killings in Florida (17 killed, 17 injured), Las Vegas (58 killed, over 500 wounded), South Carolina (9 killed), Texas (26 killed, 20 wounded) and many others since 2012.

FACT: Between 2004 and 2012, there have been 14,773 reports to the United States Food and Drug Administration's MedWatch program on psychiatric drugs causing violent side effects, including: 1,531 cases of homicidal ideation/homicide, 3,287 cases of mania and 8,219 cases of aggression.[94] Note: The FDA admits that only 1%–10% of drug side effects are reported to its MedWatch program. Taking a moderate 5%, the potential number of unreported incidents could be as high as 30,620. A percentage of those could be driven to commit violent crimes [95]

FACT: Of **409** official psychiatric drug warnings placed on prescription bottles:

49 warn of self-harm, suicide or suicidal ideation

27 warn of violence, mania, psychosis, hostility, aggression or homicidal ideation

43 warn of death or increased risk of death

35 link emotional problems to the drugs

17 warn of addiction or withdrawal effects

As the the watchdog, Citizens Commission on Human Rights, pointed out:

"If 5% of the 41 million Americans taking antidepressants were to experience 'increased' mental and/or physical agitation, that repre-

sents 2.05 million people. How many of them could potentially become so agitated that they would carry out violent acts? It's a case of playing Russian roulette with our lives." [96]

Hide the Evidence.
It's All About the Love of Money

Matthew 6:24

FACT: It took months for the release of information showing that police had found psychiatric drugs in the apartment of Aurora, Colorado, movie theater shooter, James Holmes (on March 22, 2012)...and despite official, legal requests for the release of the Sandy Hook Elementary School shooter, Adam Lanza's, toxicology reports and medical history to ascertain whether psychiatric drugs played a role in the school massacre, the office of the Connecticut Medical Examiner had refused to release this crucial information to the public, prompting a parents' rights organization to take the matter to court. Eventually it was released, but long after the shooting was being reported in the news. [97]

Mass shootings are becoming common place in our culture, particularly in the United States, yet before the 1980s mass shootings and acts of senseless violence were relatively unheard of. What changed? The best known SSRI [**S**elective **S**erotonin **R**euptake **I**nhibitor] antidepressant drug, Prozac, had not yet been invented. When it became available, it was masterfully marketed by its master of darkness as the cure-all for depression. Global pharmaceutical manufacturer, Eli Lilly and Company, made huge profits from this drug alone, which led every other drug manufacturer to create their own "Prozac." Year after year, with the advent of what has now become common place drugs, the shootings have increased.

An article published in the scientific journal, *PLOS One*, entitled, *"Antidepressants are a Prescription for Mass Shootings,"* discussed the findings of a study from the Institute of Safe Medication and stated the following:

> *"In a study of 31 drugs that are disproportionately linked to reports of violence toward others, **five** of the top 10 are antidepressants. These are Prozac, Paxil, Luvox, Effexor and Pristiq.* ***Two other drugs that are for treating ADHD are also in the top ten which means these are being given to children who could then become violent.*** *One could conclude from this study alone that antidepressants **cause** both suicidal thoughts and violent behavior [including homicidal]. This is a prescription for mass shootings."* [98]

What this comes down to is big money and power. That there are those sitting in powerful seats in these pharmaceutical companies who know that their drugs will lead to mass shootings, in which the youth are most in harm's way, is unconscionable—and the greatest act of selfishness. If anyone

poisons someone with a chemical, they would be charged with murder. Yet, those in pharmaceutical companies, who have knowledge of what their drugs do, have a license to murder by proxy, as long as they give the Black Box FDA Warning. All for the god of profit. They come up with sly words that mitigate, not alarm, by printing on the warning, homicidal ideation and suicidal ideation which is a cover up of instead saying clearly, WARNING: This drug has caused murder of self and others. Can you get away with murder? How much of these big pharmaceutical companies' massive profits are used to influence politicians and the media who will not report the facts presented here? The medical argument that the benefits for good far outweighs the risk of homicide can never be accepted to justify murder.

Big pharma was also in President Donald Trump's crosshairs because of their greed and corruption. In a speech given on August 6, 2020, in Ohio, Trump he said:

> *"I have people that I know that go to Canada — they go to Canada to buy drugs. To buy prescription drugs, they go there because the price is so much lower than the United States. And yet, it's made by the same company, often in the same plant. It's a disgrace. And the politicians allowed this to happen for many, many decades."*[99]

Trump signed an executive order that allows Americans to bypass American companies and order the same medicine at cheaper prices from other countries, giving Americans a savings of 40–70% of what they were paying here. This did not make Trump popular with Big Pharma. He evidently put himself in danger when he took on those "rich enemies" in the drug industry. He even insinuated at his talk in Ohio that they wanted him assassinated. Trump said:

"So I have a lot of enemies out there. This may be the last time you'll see me for a while. A lot of very, very rich enemies, but they are not happy with what I'm doing. But I figure we have one chance to do it, and no other president is going to do what I do. No other president would do a favored nations, a rebate, a buy from other nations at much less cost. Nobody. And there are a lot of unhappy people, and they're very rich people, and they're very unhappy."[100]

These big pharmaceutical companies have only one agenda: to make mega money no matter what they have to do. Twelve days before the school shooting in Parkland, Florida, Our Lady said this on the day for nonbelievers*:

February 2, 2018

> **"…do not permit for selfishness, for self love, to rule the world…"**

* Every second of the month is referred to as the day for nonbelievers because Our Lady, for many years, appeared on that day to Medjugorje visionary, Mirjana, and gave her a special message specifically speaking of nonbelievers. Our Lady, who always sees souls in a positive light, told Mirjana that the true definition of nonbelievers are those who have not experienced the love of God.

Our Lady also said this same day:

> **"...My children, do not believe lying voices which speak to you about false things, false light..."**

Though all school shootings are deeply troubling and sad, the shooting in Parkland seemed particularly sad—perhaps because the increase in these incidents is unrelenting. Or maybe because of the day in which it was perpetrated, Ash Wednesday, begins a 40-day period in which Christians meditate on the Passion of Jesus, through prayer and penance, repent of their sins and seek forgiveness, which leads to Easter and the celebration of Christ's Resurrection. Our Lady warns that this "way" is not easy.

February 2, 2018

> **"...I am here for the sake of love, for the sake of faith, because with my motherly blessing I desire to give you hope and strength on your way—be-**

cause the way which leads to my Son is not easy. It is full of renunciation, giving, sacrifice, forgiveness and much, much love. But this way leads to peace and happiness…"

Many reject this truth of Our Lady. Harvard professor, Steven Pinker, in an interview on February 15, 2018, the day after the attack, asked the question that many were asking: Where was God? He said, in regards to a book he wrote:

> *"It is not against religion. It is certainly against the belief that God interferes with the laws of the universe and that by praying to Him we can make the world better. I think that is a dangerous belief because it's not true. If we want to make the world better, we have to figure out how to do it ourselves."* [101]

Pinker is "so smart" that he continues to give his brilliant, arrogant answer. Instead of God and prayer, he states:

"If we want to cure disease, we have to come up with antibiotics and vaccines and ***not prayer****. If we want to stave off Global Warming, we can't assume God won't let bad things happen. Cast doubt on the idea that there is a Benevolent Shepherd who looks out for human welfare. What was the Benevolent Shepherd doing while the teenager was massacring his classmates? If you're counting on God to make the world a better place you are probably going to make the world a worse place because He is not listening and we saw that yesterday."*[102] (Referring to the Parkland, Florida, school shooting)

This is what universities, and even many schools, are propagating. Anti-prayer, anti-God, and we wonder where God is?

How far have some in this nation traveled from the strong faith and love of God that made this nation great? God is thrown out of our schools, out of our government, out of our hospitals, out of our culture, and we expect Him to protect us anyway? And if He did, would He have received the credit for it? Would CNN or most of those throughout the media call for a day of Thanksgiving to God for saving the children in Parkland, Florida, if the perpetrator of the crime was caught before the killings? We know the answer.

Darkness is in the crosshairs of Heaven now that we have entered into Our Lady's Century.* This is the meaning of the Ash Wednesday massacre. Ash Wednesday leads to Christ's victory on the Cross; His Glory followed.

* On December 26, 1982, Our Lady told Medjugorje visionary, Mirjana, that satan had requested from God a century to try the Church, and that this century, the 20th Century, was under the power of satan. Pope Leo XIII in 1887 was told the same thing in a dream. While many believed that the century of satan would end by the year 2000, with the advancement of evil starting with September 11, 2001, followed by scandals in the Church being made public, nations going to war, etc., one realized that man's century and God's century were not on the same time table. After some time passed, a more plausible explanation was conceived: that the century of satan began in and around the year 1917, the year of Our Lady's apparitions in Fatima. The conclusion of that century would then be around 2017–100 years from 1917–2017. While we continue to see evidence that satan is in control in the physical realm, in the spiritual realm we believe that behind-the-scenes events began happening in 2017 to begin dismantling satan's antichrist system. We believe we are in the death throes of his system that will come down rapidly and completely when the Secrets of Medjugorje begin to happen.

September 2, 2011

> **"... My Son has brought you, the people of the entire world, to know the only true God and His love...Therefore, my children, do not wander, do not close your heart before that truth, hope and love. Everything around you is passing and everything is falling apart, only the glory of God remains..."**

Is it not strange that Our Lady said on:

December 2, 2005

> **"Dear children, in this holy time..."**

Why would Our Lady say this is a 'holy time' with what is going on? Because Our Lady is with us. This makes this period of time holy, because Holiness descends upon the earth every day. What would we hold onto if Our Lady was not with us in this period? It would be enough to panic. Thank God we have the comfort of Her daily presence, of Her words, of Her direction. Without Her, the world would have turned into a hell. The only thing standing between the earth and hell is Our Lady. It is for this reason She comes to save the world.

August 25, 1992

> **"...I may be enabled to convert and save the world..."**

Our Lady, revealing She is here to 'save the world,' is an incomprehensible, profound revelation that the world would end if She did not come to convert it and save it.

After Our Lady no longer appears, Her messages will be the light on earth for the time that comes and through the great tribulation that will be fully under the power of the incarnate satan. Your life, your witness will become, in the future, what the elect* will follow in order to know how to survive under the great future trial in living under the

* Elect means a group of people chosen by God to do a particular task for Eternal Life.

antichrist which will usher in the Second Coming of Christ. Sounds big? Yes, Medjugorje, Our Lady's apparitions, Our Lady's messages are that big and that is why Our Lady said:

January 25, 1987

> **"...You are not able to comprehend how great your role is..."**

Your role is to be active now, because your role transitions into the lives of billions who will come after you. You question that? Look at the few who walked with Jesus. Throughout all these past centuries, billions of Christians were affected by the lives of those few. When Our Lady said on January 25, 1987, **"...you cannot comprehend... your role..."** that means you will not, no more than those early Christians could possibly grasp how great their role would be in the plan of salvation. Do not hold back on Medjugorje. Go into it with all you have and are.

"During a decade in elected office in Indiana, I made it my practice while traveling the state to stay overnight in Hoosier homes rather than hotels. Because of geography and, candidly, personal choice, probably a third of those 125 overnights were with farm families. There I witnessed virtues that one sees too rarely these days–hard work, practical manual skill, a communitarian ethic–woven tightly into the fabric of everyday life."[103]

Mitch Daniels
Former Governor of Indiana

CHAPTER NINE

What Really is A.D.D.?
You Will Get the Answer.

We are producing youth today who have very limited capabilities. We allowed an educational system to be created in which the primary goal is school attendance. Graduate and you are qualified for employment. Lie, lie, lie. Most youth within the modern educational system do nothing of substance and what achievements they do accomplish are with little to no value. What does that do to their self-esteem and confidence?

Question: What animal kills the most people in the world?

Answer: Farm animals!

You learn a lot, a whole lot of wisdom around farm animals. You learn almost everything you will need in life, mainly common sense, which is the highest intelligence one can obtain. Our Lady said:

December 2, 2007

> **"...God's Word which is the light of salvation and the light of common sense."**

Jesus was the Word and the Word became Flesh. It is amazing that Our Lady put these two things together; salvation and common sense, defining what the "Word" is. Common sense is far superior to intellectualism, which is often not "logical." Jesus was not a theologian. Jesus was "The" "logical" Man begotten by God. God "is" "Theo" "logical."* Man has strayed from what is common sense and no longer is theologically based. Man is rootless and has adapted intellectualism debased from a "logical" common sense. On one particular morning, Pope Francis had

* "Theo" literally means relating to God or deities.

spent several hours with theologians. After his Mass, an old woman spoke to him for a few minutes. He said he heard more profound things in a few minutes from her than he had heard the whole morning from all the theologians put together.

The "thing" the world is into is "education." Because "education" has turned into an evil focus, it leads to an attitude of entitlement when one believes that by holding a piece of paper (a diploma), one is entitled to a job. Yet, what if the new graduate is less adept to fill the job than one who has been trained through apprenticeship, who actually is able to do the work of a professional, who with common sense, would be more qualified than one holding a piece of paper saying they deserve the job? What if the one who only graduated from high school is more capable than the one who graduated from college? Apprenticeship is the best education no matter what field you want to be in.

Today's youth are handicapped by going from first grade to twelfth grade, doing nothing but studying books and taking tests. They graduate knowing next to nothing in skills. What the youth have lost is the agrarian way of life. The agrarian way of life is an outside classroom, filled with bountiful lessons that teach life skills, virtue, common sense and the love of God, family and country. One of the greatest virtues to form in your children is a strong work ethic. The agrarian way of life teaches this naturally. It will also teach you how to raise your children. If you have animals that you raise, you will learn how to raise kids. I thank God I got into horses when I was young. I was 14 when I began working with horses. I learned methods of discipline with horses that I applied in disciplining and raising my own children which now also guides how our children in community learn.

This void that we experience in the world today, was created by the separation of society from the agrarian way of life. The distance from which we have grown from the soil is one of the major tragedies that exists in our time. We need to go back to an agrarian way of life, because it is necessary for man. It is not an option. Why? Because it is cored in the very humanness of man when God ordained for man, ***"By the sweat of your brow shall you eat."*** (Genesis 3:19) God did not say "maybe" by the sweat of your brow, but rather, "by" the sweat of your brow. Man is to toil the soil. Not in poverty, in the sense that if you are poor, you are forced to work the soil. And not in a way that it is not consoling. To be close to the land brings something from the soil that is satisfying to the soul of man. It is something that man feels grateful for because he can see and feel God's blessings and providence.

A study was done recently on human emotions and horses. The researchers discovered that if the trainer looked at a horse with anger, the horse would do a sideways glance towards its left side, which gives a more sinister appearance. They have pictures of people making faces or smiling at the horses, and of all the 28 horses studied, every one could identify the differences. When a face showed anger, the horses' heart rates would increase, their attention would be different, and they reacted with nervousness. When a man, emotionally connected to a horse, made an angry face, every horse could "read" that emotion, regardless of the horse![104] For what purpose did God put these traits into the DNA of horses? Because God would ordain, for millenniums, that man and horses would be working together.

This is an amazing discovery! This knowledge, of course, is very useful in training horses and helps the trainer to become one with the horse. The knowledge of these and other traits, of what the animal kingdom has within it that connects to and forms harmony between man and animal, has been lost. This is different from what people and organizations like P.E.T.A. (People for the Ethical Treatment of Animals) profess. They worship the animal rather than its Maker. Many lessons about life, raising a family and developing a strong work ethic come from raising animals, and growing one's own food. There is a great void in today's society, because so few are raised in an agrarian life that provides children the possibility to be around animals and the soil, reaping from it what one produces with one's own hands. Consequently, there are so many joys that children miss out on in life as well as valuable lessons that will help them overcome any adversity they face in their adult lives.

I am the father of seven, six boys, the last one is a girl. One of my sons lives in Texas. Another one is in Florida. Both train horses. They both use two different methods of training. One trains on the ground before even getting on the horse. The other breaks the horse by mounting it and riding the horse out. The one in Texas called me the other day and said he got on a horse that was four years old that hadn't been ridden much. The trainer my son is working with is very well known in taking wild two-year-olds and breaking them in, so that other trainers can begin training them. My son got on one horse, and the horse just exploded underneath him. It bucked for over 100 yards. My son is so conditioned to riding these horses that he doesn't get thrown off. I asked, 'Did it scare you?' He said, 'No, I loved it.' He is gaining skills that you can never get at a university or anywhere else in life, except dealing with animals like this. It is dangerous. It is deadly. But these skills and experiences will help him in all kinds of circumstances that will come up in his life.

The man he works with has been injured seriously several times. Doctors have had to put his face back together, and that was when he had been working horses already about 30 years. I always tell my son, 'You say a "Hail Mary" before you get on these horses,' because he is jumping on a stick of dynamite; they are explosive the way they ride. My son rides until he calms the horse down, and then he passes it on to somebody to refine it further in training. Not many people want to get on an atomic bomb. These horses are high-strung, very well bred and very expensive, so they are keyed up 10 times more than a normal wild horse would be.

The point being made is to see how we are missing something in life. One might say, "I don't want my son on a stick of dynamite," but that's not the point being made. It's about esteem and confidence in which he learns, *"I can handle any challenge, even if I don't know what to do because common sense is my guiding light."* That can translate into their lives that Christ is their guiding light. As Our Lady categorized the two: **"...light of salvation and light of common sense..."**

People do not have an infrastructure to properly raise their children from infants to young adults, even if they want to do it. The infrastructure doesn't exist! That is why villages have to begin springing up again. That is why people have to go back to the land and live a life close to the soil. They have to get back to raising animals and food. The agrarian village life will teach everything youth need to deal with life. With that foundation base, they will be able to learn anything.

The vanquishing of the agrarian way of life hurts children. They are "minused" out of work. In the state of Alabama, there has been a recent push by governmental authorities to start enforcing child labor laws. It is insane. Those laws were passed for abuses taking place in sweatshops of manufacturers a century ago, especially in big cities like New York. Their purpose was to prevent people from taking advantage of children. There is a major difference between sweatshops and teaching your child when they are young to love work. Why would you not want your five-year-old daughter to learn and contribute to the work in keeping your household in order—like helping wash dishes, dusting furniture, putting away her clothes, or making her bed? Or if you have a company, wouldn't you want to begin to pass on to your young son those skills you worked your lifetime to gain? It is frightening to contemplate what that kind of stupidity would lead to in our society. There are people out there who do not even believe that a child under the age of 16 should be working in any aspect. So, will they suddenly, at age 16, want to start working? Donald Trump was with his dad, going with him to work at a very young age. He learned how to work and developed skills not available anywhere else. His children did the same, following him around job sites. They all grew up loving to work and are all very successful and high achievers.

Government authorities are actually pursuing parents who bring their children to their work. They are going in and checking on these places. For instance, if a mother has a clothing store, in some states, they want to make it illegal for her fourteen year old to fold clothes for her. Recently, an official enforcing these child labor laws, stated that a child cannot do anything under the age of 16 that benefits the business. So, if you have your child at work with you, and you tell little Johnny or little Suzie to sweep the floor, are you going to get arrested? What has happened to us?! Where is logic? Where is reason? Where is common sense?

In The Gospel as Revealed to Me,* Italian mystic, Maria Valtorta, tells of St. Joseph[105] teaching Jesus, at five years old, how to make little useful things for His Mother in his carpentry shop. Joseph, a master carpenter not only was passing onto Jesus the skills of carpentry, but was showing Jesus how to love His Mother through the presents He makes and brings to Her. In today's world without common sense, officials are saying this type of work is equivalent to working in a sweatshop. If they do

* This book was formerly known as The Poem of the Man God. See footnote in Chapter 3, page 31.

not desist, parents are actually being threatened with fines and jail time.

The Community of Caritas is well-known for the way their children work and grow up here. The children are constantly around community members in their work. It is play for them. The adults work while the children play around them. The children are encouraged to help whether in the mission or at home. One example shows this clearly. I had two of my grandchildren in my kitchen. Lucy was four and 'little' Tony was two. I was washing the dishes and cleaning things up after lunch. They wanted to help, but I only had an hour for lunch and I knew they would get in the way. I had a lot going on, a fully-packed day. But they wanted to wash dishes. I didn't hesitate. I let them help me. I pulled up their sleeves and put them both on a stool by the sink. They made a big mess. There was water all over the place. But they enjoyed helping me. Lucy was continually correcting Tony, saying

'No, Tony,' because he was taking the dishes that I had just washed and that she had just rinsed throwing them back into the soapy water. She kept telling him to stop. I said, 'Let him do what he's doing, Lucy. For him, he thinks he's working.' It was a joy to see that. If you could have been peeking behind a corner, you couldn't help but smile. I was smiling. Yes, it was a situation that you could be aggravated with or impatient. But, I took it the other way, and it became a grace for me and for them. After we were finished, little Tony got down from the stool and just folded his arms like he had done something big. I had to wipe the floor up. Water was all over the counters. I also had to rinse everything again.

Most people won't do that, but these are life's lessons of learning that work is fun. It was more difficult to allow them to do that than for me to just get the work done. But it was not as important that I get my work done on my timetable, as it was to take the time to teach about work to the second and third generation coming up behind me. It is also about **'how'** you get your work done, and **'what'** you do with it, and the **'fruit'** from it that is most important than just getting it done. I would ask the question to adults about their work and if they are making it valuable. How? What? Fruit?

We have people making terrible, terrible mistakes. They do not know how to raise or create a healthy environment for their children. We have broken parents raising broken youth. It is like broken people shooting broken arrows. Not only do they not hit the target, they miss the target every time. Kids today have never been taught the many things that most kids grew up knowing in the past. The preoccupation with electronics are destroying the youth and in the end, what seems prosperous is a mirage. The modern ways of today's world will vanish, leaving nothing of value behind for the future of the world. It is going to fall apart because it does not glorify God. Only what glorifies God will remain.

What then will people do without any skills to take care of themselves, feed themselves, etc.? I am not going out on a limb by saying this. You who reject it are the ones who are out on a limb by not pondering this prediction. The billions of hours that people have spent and will continue to spend on cell phones will be for them as bitter hot coals on their tongues. A catastrophic loss of time. One will eventually realize how they blocked the voice of God by being preoccupied with the little cell phone god instead of the Almighty Being, God Himself. God could never get a prompt or word in, not a single WORD, to warn you that you must change the direction of your life to become agrarian. The words of cell phones—the WORD of God. Who is going to win?

Recently we were told by a parent, *"Well, I have to have those fidget spinners for my kids to keep them busy like a babysitter."* Her child is just three years old. Go ahead, and see what kind of monster you end up with at 14. Here at Caritas, we have our three-year-olds learning how to work and expend their energy which calms them down—not with drugs. They may be making a mess, but that will not stop us from keeping them here with us by our side. But, there will be many adults who will have a lot of problems in life because they never learned the things they needed to learn in their childhood. We live a tragedy in our culture because of this. Look at the youth, the schools, the fruit and the resulting state of the family.

Our Lady is here to teach us holiness and conversion. Who is Our Lady? What kind of Woman is She? She is the one that is here to show us, *"I want your children working through play."* Why? Because a good work ethic is holy. Children have to learn how to work when they are young to be happy when they grow older. If they do not have that, they will be idle with stupid TV, electronic games, etc. In ages past, we know from those "mean ol' full-habited" nuns from grammar school, for those of us that were taught their wisdom, that they always said, *"Idleness is the devil's workshop."* And truly, that is where much sin comes from; being too idle because they never learned the value and satisfaction of work.

This chapter title asks the question, What Really is A.D.D.? The answer is:

Agrarian **D**eficit **D**isorder

The **A**ttention **D**eficit **D**isorder, or the upgraded **A**ttention **D**eficit/**H**yperactivity **D**isorder is a lie, a manufactured illness, created by a lie by pharmaceutical companies who profit from the drugs they produce to treat the fake illness (Ritalin, Adderall etc.). What makes pharmaceutical companies any different from drug dealers on the street or from the drug cartel? What difference is there in the lives that are destroyed on the streets by narcotics to the ones who are addicted to psychotropic drugs in the classroom? None. Which leads to an important question. Who is the most responsible for many of the shootings today? The school shooter pulling the trigger or the manufacturer of the suicidal and murderous drugs? It may be hard to accept this, but the reality is that shooters are victims themselves.

The **A**grarian **D**eficit **D**isorder is a true disorder and the medicine that will cure it is an agrarian-based life, among other solutions that will be discussed in later chapters.* The earth is groaning in birth pains, to beget a new world. You will be in one of two camps, at its birth. One will rejoice. One will lament. Our Lady said on August 25, 1997:

> **"...God gives me this time...to...instruct and lead you...now you do not comprehend...but soon a time will come when you will lament for these messages..."**

* In regards to understanding what Heaven is trumpeting to the earth at this spiritual and historical moment, you can learn about Heaven's mandates through a book titled, The Corona Vision. See the order form in the back of this book.

"Children don't have disorders; they live in a disordered world."[106]

Peter R. Breggins M.D.
Psychiatrist

CHAPTER TEN

Kids are Raised Like Veal

What is veal? Veal is a calf that is killed when it is young. These calves are only fed with milk and are kept inside an area where they are not allowed to move around. This is because it keeps the meat tender. Many times when the calves are let out to bring them to be slaughtered, they stumble and fall because they are kept inactive for so long. [107] This is what today's kids are, especially when glued to electronics. They are like veal. They don't have any constructive stamina. They haven't made any real accomplishments outside of school and sports. Schools are all about good grades, which youth are praised for. Is that an accomplishment? When I was in the third grade, I made on my report card 72 D's and 13 F's. I flunked the third grade. It didn't bother my self-esteem. I didn't have a meltdown. Why? I was joyful for being put back in the third grade because I liked the kids better coming into the third grade the following year. I also knew I would be the oldest in my class. I played alot in school and didn't do homework, which didn't help me earn good grades on my report card. But, I spent alot of time in the school library reading about so many different topics, the things I enjoyed learning about. While in high school and later when I graduated, I ended up building a very successful business and by God's grace, the very successful mission of Caritas of Birmingham. I was proud of my accomplishments in school because they strengthened me, making me thick-skinned. I didn't care what anyone thought of me and I knew I was so much more than the grades given on a report card.

Lenore Skenazy is the president of "Let Grow," a nonprofit promoting childhood independence and resilience. She is also the founder of the Free-Range Kids movement and coauthored with Jonathan Haidt, the article:*"The Fragile Generation: Bad Policy and Paranoid Parenting are Making Kids Too Safe to Succeed."* In this article they discuss what happens when we raise children like veal and rob them of the opportunities that they need to become responsible, dependable, successful adults with common sense and self-control. Skenazy and Haidt state:

> *"When we raise kids unaccustomed to facing anything on their own, including risk, failure, and hurt feelings, our society, and even our economy are threatened…"* [108]

Bullying was never a major issue in past generations. Kids learned how to deal with it. Don't be a crybaby. Toughen up. Now, because bullying has been made a mortal sin and the greatest injustice, youth have become snowflakes. * Children and older youth are not learning how to cope with adversities or words that hurt their "veal" feelings. This is part of life, youth must learn how to deal with them without feeling they may die because of these antics. In times' past, youth would have been told by an adult, *"Get over it,"* or *"Let it roll off your back,"* like water rolls off the back of a duck. Why are we not teaching our children what older generations were taught, that made them tough and protected them from becoming too sensitive? Another proverbial saying full of wisdom that was taught to previous generations, but not today, is:

> *"Sticks and stones may break my bones, but words will never hurt me."*

What did Our Lady say to the visionaries when they were being severely persecuted?

* The term "snowflakes" was attached to millennials because whenever someone hurts their feelings, they melt like a snowflake.

June 27, 1981

> **"My angels, do not be afraid of injustices. They have always existed."**

In other words, Our Lady is saying accept it, get over it, and move on. In fact, She just said this in a recent message:

July 25, 2022

> **"...You be joyful witnesses of God's word and love, and with hope in the heart which conquers every evil. Forgive those who inflict evil on you, and go on the way of holiness..."**

Skenazy and Haidt continue in, "The Fragile Generation."

> *"How did we come to think a generation of kids can't handle the basic challenges of growing up?...*

"Beginning in the 1980s, American childhood changed…children largely lost the experience of having large swaths of unsupervised time to play, explore, and resolve conflicts on their own. This has left them more fragile, more easily offended, and more reliant on others. They have been taught to seek authority figures to solve their problems and shield them from discomfort…

"This poses a threat to the kind of open-mindedness and flexibility young people need to thrive. If they arrive at school or start careers unaccustomed to frustration and misunderstandings, we can expect them to be hyper-sensitive. And if they don't develop the resources to work through obstacles, molehills come to look like mountains…" [109]

The young Medjugorje visionaries went through savage treatment, not just by nonbelievers, but by Communist police who threatened to kill them and harm their families. Our Lady's advice to them was always for them to bear it, accept it.

June 29, 1981

> **"...Do not fear. You will be able to endure everything. You must believe and have confidence in me."**

This message contradicts all the advice being given to youth today. Endure EVERY-THING. But, instead of coping and dealing with adversity, youth can legally go to amphetamines such as "Adderall" or "Ritalin." Doped up, life is easier to handle, it soothes their emotions as they become more listless. Again, from "The Fragile Generation":

> *"If you're over 40, chances are good that you had scads of free time as a child after school, on weekends, over the summer. And chances are also good that if you were asked about it now, you'd go on and on about playing in the*

woods and riding your bike until the street-lights came on...

"Today, many kids are raised like veal. Only 13 percent of them even walk to school...

"Kids learn by doing. Trip over a tree stump, and you learn to look down. There's an old saying, 'Prepare your child for the path, not the path for your child.' We're doing the opposite..." [110]

In the days when people borrowed some butter, sugar, etc., from their neighbors, moms would not drive their kids in the car two or four houses down the street. Kids were expected to walk, be it hot or cold, rain or snow or through the mud. Youth must do hard things to learn how to do things that challenge them when they grow up. With purpose, children and teenagers should not be allowed to take the easy path. Learning hardships makes life easier. Our Lady, Herself, challenged

Her young visionaries and the youth prayer groups to do hard things.

Medjugorje visionary, Marija, told a story about when Our Lady was in need of a special sacrifice for an intention She wanted realized. She asked Marija and the prayer group to climb Cross Mountain late one night. It was winter time. Freezing cold. Dark. The bone-chilling Bora winds* that course across the region in the winter time were blowing. Marija said that she was wearing a skirt that night. When the prayer group started the climb, it was raining, turning the dirt on the paths into slippery mud. For one who has been on Cross Mountain in Medjugorje, you will know that these kind of conditions make it not only difficult to climb, they make it dangerous because the rocks are very slippery. And yet Our Lady said to do it! To top it all off, it was a school night, and Our Lady told them not to take any

* A constant wind, without gusts. A steady wind of 40–50 mph with no let up for days.

flashlights! How many mothers today would ask their children to do that? What would you say if you heard that your neighbor had told her children to do such a thing? [111]

When the prayer group neared the Tenth Station of the Cross on Cross Mountain, Our Lady suddenly appeared and gave a special grace. Everyone in the prayer group got to hear Our Lady's voice when She told them that the penance the prayer group had done to this point was sufficient, and they could return home without completing the rest of the climb. Our Lady had accomplished Her objective through the penance of the prayer group.

Why such harshness? Isn't that cruel? No. Our Lady has wisdom. Skenazy is in agreement, again quoting from"The Fragile Generation":

> *"Play is training for adulthood. Not letting your child climb a tree because he might fall,*

robs him of a classic childhood experience. But being emotionally overprotective takes away something else. We have realized a generation of young people who have not been given the opportunity to experience failure and realize they can survive it…

"We have stolen from children the best resilience training known to man: free play…

"'Free play is the means by which children learn to make friends, overcome their fears, solve their own problems, and generally take control of their own lives,' Gray writes in 2013 Free to Learn. *'Nothing we do, no amount of toys we buy, or quality time, or special training we give our children, can compensate for the freedom we take away. The things that children learn through their own initiatives in free play cannot be taught in other ways'…*

"Unstructured, unsupervised time for play is one of the most important things we have to give back to kids if we want them to be strong and happy and resilient." [112]

In Our Lady's Community of Caritas, good fruit came from how my wife and I raised our children:

"Our kids are free range, free play. They do it all day from morning to dark. The biggest complaint they can have is, if they're sick, and they can't go up across the road, or they can't go outside and play with the other kids. Their day can be filled with joy, injuries, hurts, cuts, stitches, happiness, fun, and broken bones. While it is true that we don't allow them to do something completely reckless, we don't protect them from negative consequences they receive in normal play and work. But our kids have agility simply because they are able to do things most parents would never let their kids do. This has taught our kids to be astute,

watchful, careful and smart. It has taught them to be leaders, not followers."

Another no-no for us in Community: **we don't put our kids in a car to go to the grocery store, Walmart runs, etc. Why expose them to going here and there when they could be playing within the Community or even working. Every minute away from the Community is lost cognition of many continuous experiences. When a mom goes grocery shopping, etc., there is no reason to have a child go with them when it is not necessary. It is not constructive for the youth.**

The Community is structured in such a way that young children can be looked after by older youth and adults. Their playhouse is *The Tabernacle of Our Lady's Messages* (the mission building of Caritas of Birmingham) and the grounds surrounding it. We realize that not everyone is so blessed where they can leave their children any time on a minute's notice with people they know and trust.

But, we made changes in our lives to make this a part of our way of life. Parents and grandparents should look to how they can do the same. At least, start minimizing the number of trips you take your child with you. God will bless your efforts and your prayers for this intention. The only time community children go out on an errand or shopping trip is if someone is going to a tractor or equipment store, a farm co-op, the stock yards, etc., which is useful for the child's learning. Most everything else is frivolous, useless, and even damaging to the youth as it wets their appetite for the world and materialism the more they are exposed to it.

The purpose of this chapter, "Kids are Raised Like Veal," is to bring about a change of mentality regarding what society is steering youth towards. You as parents, teachers, pastors, grandparents, etc., are to contradict this mentality of rearing children never having to experience adversity. Adversity teaches children how to overcome the walls that block them from advancing in life. When there are no setbacks, there are also no experiences of victory in overcoming all kinds of adversities. We have created a selfish, self-centered culture that rather than building strong character and resiliency in our youth, is building a nanny state of dependents who believe they are being deprived of rights whenever they are denied what they want.

It is easy to see that we are raising an entire generation focused on self. The cell phone craze of "take a selfie," epitomizes the sickness in our culture of being so self absorbed as to be oblivious to the world around you. It is a symptom, not of self-confidence, but actually of low self-esteem. Low self-esteem contributes to low resilience, which can lead to frustration and depression. It also leads to blaming everyone else for the bad things that happen to you as well as an "everyone is against me" attitude. Add drugs to the situation and it all adds up to the warning label, "homicidal ideation," the "cover-up" name to soften what its true meaning is and what the label should be changed to say clearly, as already stated: **"This drug has caused murder to self and to others."**

The theme threaded through Our Lady's messages is "don't think of self, rather think of neighbor." Not what they can do for you, but what you can do for them. All these lessons, such as the Community adults looking after the children while mom goes shopping, is doing good to our neighbor. We give to each other. The environment the children are exposed to, the witness of looking after each other, makes it natural for the children to grow up with the same faith we practice, looking out for others rather than self, which rains down blessings on us all. Our Lady said:

February 2, 2018

> **"...do not permit selfishness, for self love, to rule the world...When you are**

giving yourself for the faith, when you are giving yourself for love, when you are doing good to your neighbor, my Son smiles in your soul..."

As you have read these points, our solution is a simple answer. What is not simple, is turning solutions into physical reality. You must pray. Pray and make changes toward your whole approach to life in regards to what the culture offers to you. Reject it and change your direction. Our Lady said:

March 25, 1990

"...change the direction of your life..."

"Back to the days of going to work on the farm or just having to work for your next meal is the new prescription for better health. Between kids getting pampered and drug companies bombarding us hourly with TV commercials is a prime cause."[113]

K.S.

Reno, Nevada

CHAPTER ELEVEN

Cattle Handling Facilities

We live in a world of things that many think are good. However, many things are not good, nor right. Our Lady says:

August 25, 1992

> **"...there is much sin and 'many things' that are evil..."**

How can things be evil? It is people who are evil. To understand that things can be evil, as Our Lady stated, you must first recognize problems in the culture. What are some of the **"things"** that have created the problems? One problem that has become a major crisis is—we have lost from times past, how to raise children in the correct way. While more and more people are coming to recognize this, the infrastructure no longer exists throughout our culture to be able to raise children correctly. What one "thing" is foremost responsible for this? Schools have gone away from one-room schoolhouses and instead followed man's efficiencies in the market place. Schools have turned into factory assembly lines of mass production. This mentality of "assembly line mass production" is pervasive in cultures across the world and is generally applied to everything. The drive behind the mentality is to turn out every product or thing with higher and higher production.

School buildings have anywhere from several hundred to 3,000 or more students. These places are nothing more than cattle handling facilities. **Mass production educational facilities are an evil because of what comes from them**, yet they are accepted without question and are seen as a good. No one questions the evolved system we now have throughout the educational system. The system is a "lying voice." Our Lady said:

February 2, 2018

"...do not believe lying voices..."

Compared to one-room schoolhouses of the past, students educated in mass production educational systems cannot hold a candle to students educated in very small schoolhouses or those who have been homeschooled.

In a test of university students, to see their educational aptitude compared to Eighth grade students from the late 1800s, an amazing result showed who are the more educated. The university students were given an Eighth grade exam from 1895. Not one single university student passed the Eighth grade test![114] So what is the educational system doing to the youth today? Answer: Severely damaging the youth, and thereby their future, the future of our nation and the future of the world.

We are growing a world society in which everything has been placed on the altar of the god of education. Our Lady said:

April 20, 2018

"...I desire to educate you, teach you..."

If our educational system is so great, why is a Superior Being, full of wisdom, sent from Heaven to say, **"... '<u>I</u>' will educate you** [and] **teach you?..."** This is an indictment against our educational system, which shows itself to be a "thing" that is evil, just as Our Lady said, **"...there are...'many things' that are evil..."** It is no secret that the whole system is a breeding ground for propagating godless humanist thinking.

What about Christian schools? One can find some good in them. However, they copy and imitate the world without recognizing they are following a path that lends itself to darkness. Darkness influences Christian education to the world's ways of operating. First, they are following the pattern of the "things" of the world. Secondly, are the students in Christian schools any more successful in passing the 1895 Eighth Grade Final Exam from a little red schoolhouse in Salina, Kansas? A great many Christian schools use the same textbooks as public schools. So what have they learned and for what good? *"You can mass produce education, but you cannot mass produce good education."*

Thirty or so years ago, a new school was being built in a nearby town. This was before the start of school shootings and many other major troubles we now face in our schools today. I was with my young sons, driving past the almost completed facility which the school board, alumni, educators and parents were so very proud of. I slowed the car to a stop, pointed to the school and said to my kids, *"This is nothing but a cattle facility. This is built on the premise of handling cattle."* Then I explained why. How is it that no one saw this back then? An even bigger question: Why do people not see it now? Because of a lack of wisdom, resulting from a lack of prayer and reflection. Our culture has become more and more "dumbed down," carried away by thoughtlessness and lack of reflection, thereby, accepting everything that offers the latest and greatest invention for the sake of efficiency. Our Lady said:

October 2, 2009

> **"…As I look at you, my heart seizes with pain. Where are you going my children? Have you sunk so deeply into sin that you do not know how to stop yourself? You justify yourselves with sin and live according to it…"**

Upon writing this chapter about handling cattle vs. students, I researched how many cows are calculated in a feedlot. I discovered this astounding revelation through my research. On a cattle feedlot facility, when speaking of how many cows are located on one acre of land, the ratio typically is 100 cows per acre in each feedlot.[115] Applying this method to our children in today's schools, they were found to use the same method. The number of kids per acre in a school typically is about 100 kids per acre. What must also be determined is when the "cattle facility" or "school" is too small to "feed" the number of minds, you are to upgrade to a larger cattle handling facility. Study the 2002 findings of **The KnowledgeWorks Foundation** from their research article, *"Dollars and Sense: The Cost Effectiveness of Small Schools,"* and see how it parallels exactly the numbers of animals per feedlot vs. the number of children per classroom:

Efficiency Determines

The Students [Feedlot] Category

Calculates to 100 Students Per Acre

10 Acres	Up to 1,000 [Animals] Elementary School Students
20 Acres	1,001–2,000 [Animals] Middle School Students.
30 Acres	2,001–3,000 [Animals] High School Students[116]

Do you protest, saying, "How dare you call students animals!" That's the point. Our children are **not** animals. It is you who have accepted children to be dealt with like animals. Our children possess human flesh. They each possess a soul, yet their souls are becoming more and more a reflection of an animal rather than of a child formed in the Image of God. The Virgin said:

October 2, 2017

> **"...My children, care for your soul, because it alone is what truly belongs to you..."**

There is nothing elevating in the school systems today. There is less and less good coming from them. They are the designs of darkened minds, and Christians are among them, those who themselves have been educated by the world's ways and adapted to them without question, even Christian schools. While Protestant schools are only a little better than most schools, they still fall short, while Catholic schools are far lower than many Protestant schools. Do you reject this statement as opinion? You are rejecting truth. Our Lady is here to enlighten us to all erred mentalities.

February 2, 2012

"...And you, my children? You continue to be deaf and blind as you look at the world around you and do not want to see where it is going without my Son. You are renouncing Him - and He is the source of all graces. You listen to me while I am speaking to you,

but your hearts are closed and you are not hearing me. You are not praying to the Holy Spirit to illuminate you. My children, pride has come to rule…"

Let's go back 50 years ago, from 2022, and read what Ven. Archbishop Fulton Sheen said:

> *"If you want your children to fight for their faith, send them to 'public school.' If you want them to lose their faith, send them to Catholic school."*[117]

But…but…but…there are good teachers, good people! Look through the glasses of Holy Scripture and Our Lady's messages to find the truth. Repeat the following sentence until it is stuck in your head in order to see correctly. It was told to me in a meeting with Cardinal Alfonso Lopez Trujillo at the Vatican:

> *"Many good people are doing bad things."*

If you get this in your mind, you will see there are "many evil things" that good people are doing, joining with, accepting, even funding. This is why Our Lady is here. Our culture is participating in fostering evil with many who are in the Church. It is necessary to repeat here, for the fourth time, why Our Lady says, **"I desire to educate you, to teach you,"** to imprint it in your heart and mind. Why? Because we are not truly educated. We are not being taught what is real, what is necessary. Some may think that is not the case, believing we are in fact being educated.

Many may object that you cannot just blankly condemn these schools! No one has to. It is self-evident as the system condemns itself. They are condemned; they are not of God. **THEY WILL PASS AWAY. THEY WILL FALL APART.** They do not glorify God. One of their many failures is that they standardize everything. Every student must conform in an unnatural way. Any nail sticking up, they hammer down with Ritalin and other drugs, instead of channeling a student's energy into a positive good. And what happens to these souls? Many end up with a negative life; a life of dependency, depression, low self-esteem and other problems, all in combination with society's family problems. Making all kids fit into the "efficiency box" is only part of the problem these cattle-handling facilities foster. Yes, there are expected behavior "norms" that all children should comply with. However, what is being discussed here, and what is happening in today's schools, is not based on normal.

We are coming into a new era, the era of Mary. The Mother who taught the Son, God Himself. There is no virtue in the infrastructure of the school system today. Where is the evidence? Go back before the Columbine High School shooting which began these events. Go back 23 years ago (from 2022) to 1999. Go back to the **United States Department of Education 1999 statistics.** What will you find when you compare small schools, with just a few hundred students enrolled, to large schools with a thousand students or more? The answer is shocking.

Six Great Problems Found in Large Schools:

1. They have 270 % more vandalism than small schools!
2. They have 378 % more theft and larceny than small schools!
3. They have 394 % more physical fighting and attacks than small schools!
4. They have 825 % more violent crime than small schools!
5. They have **1,000 %** more weapons incidents than small schools!
6. They have **3,200 %** more robberies than small schools![118]

If this is 23 years ago, how high are the percentages in 2022? An aside to this is, as a result of the "efficiencies" that brought about large schools, shooters are enabled in having large numbers of targets, while being able to hide themselves in large crowds.

Conditioned mentalities are difficult to change. The problems that developed resulted from the way we mindlessly accepted and built a system of evil and then continue to support it and participate in it everyday. How many of you are aware that fewer and fewer schools are teaching students how to read and write in cursive? I recently met a man who works for Mercedes-Benz car manufacturer in an important position. He confessed that despite his successful career, he cannot read cursive writing because it was no longer taught in school. Many students are graduating who cannot read cursive writing. That means they cannot read the original documents of the Declaration of Independence, the United States Constitution and other important historical documents of our nation's founding. Hordes of students are graduating today and are not able to read many things in history that were written in cursive. Not knowing the past, they will have no idea, therefore, of where to go in the future. We all know the saying, *"Those who forget the past are condemned to repeat it."* Is this an agenda? Or is it just following the way of efficiency mindlessly? It is both. It is an agenda of those who want to change our nation and the world. It is also mindlessness on our part allowing efficiency to rule us to our ruin.

Some may argue that it is not necessary to learn cursive anymore. Anyone can read the Constitution in English print in many books. But, that is exactly the problem. A prevalent agenda of Leftist historians is to revise the history of our nation, in order to redefine what it means to be an American and what our nation was birthed to be. As more and more 'educated people' cannot read cursive, they will read revisionist books and teachings and will not be able to compare it to the original writings in cursive. The reader can be easily indoctrinated by not knowing how to read cursive.

Do you think there is too much being made on this one point, even an exaggeration of it? Ask yourself first, why stop teaching cursive in the first place? First, it is the continuing degradation of our language so future generations will not know what our Forefathers intended when they created this nation. Second, anyone can look at the published books of recent years and find abundant historical revisions. Revisionism and lies are saturated in a wide variety of topics in publishing today to change what and who we are as a people.

What does this have to do with large vs. small schools? If a small school initiates progressive agendas, parents can easily stop it. However, when a system is institutionalized, parents have little power or influence. Large sizes break down the power and influence of parents; parents can then be handled like cattle, without being able to object with influence to stop a bad policy. One can see this by observing recent school board meetings across the nation.

School boards, using dictatorship power, mow over parents who object to policies that the school has put into place. Often these policies are ideological, indoctrinating children with extreme leftist views. The result is that one must accept what the institution decides. The larger the school, the more rules and the less human they become. Larger schools not only result in students being regulated and controlled, but also the parents' behavior is being regulated and controlled. Don't think the P.T.A. (Parent Teacher Association) works for you. For the most part, it has become a forum to control parents and manage them. In reality, parents have no say on how schools run. There is only a pretense of townhall-type meetings that make parents think they have input. A call for meetings, time to time, lets the parent get off their chest what they object to, then the institution does what they themselves decide.

In the article, "Dollars and Sense: The Cost Effectiveness of Small Schools," it is stated that:

> *"Large size and fragmented human contact complicate the management of large schools, which elevates the importance of formal rules to regulate behavior, [therefore], the environment in comprehensive high schools is…less human."*[119]

As schools become smaller and smaller, there is less need of regulating behavior and rules. As schools become larger, the opposite is true. Parents are empowered by a small school system, as it makes it easier for parents and their beliefs to influence the one room type schoolhouse, as opposed to the large schools which fragment and control parental influence. The smaller the school the better the school.

But even the smaller conventional schools fall short of what students need.

Long ago, I coined the term, *"creeping gradualism."** It is satan's tactic to creep unnoticed with his agenda, gradually implementing his radical plan and deceptions which are never noticed until it's too late. By the time his schemes are noticed, society at large has already given the green light, first through tolerance, and second, through acceptance without resistance or rejection. This is how schools evolved into evil systems of cattle-handling facilities that are not only accepted, but respected as good. This is true even though schools are propagating many evil things today. Dr. Stuart Grauer, founder of the lauded, Grauer School, that is based in experiential education, and which leads the small schools movement, stated in an essay:

* A Friend of Medjugorje has introduced verbiage that has entered the English language, such as "creeping gradualism." Another example of a phrase he coined, is the "physical realm vs. the spiritual realm." These and other phrases over the course of decades, have been adopted by many other people, even those on popular talk shows.

"Like many of our cities, the large school model had evolved very gradually and was not the result of a set plan, and so no one could state a single place or point in time where a threshold had been crossed…"[120]

Recall in the first chapter, how falsehood goes through three phases:

1. It is accepted.
2. It is challenged.
3. It causes confusion.

This writing is a call to **challenge** the falsehood of today's educational system. It will cause **confusion,** forcing each person to choose one of the following three camps to belong to:

1. Those who believe large schools are good.

vs.

2. Those who recognize the truth of small schoolhouses.

vs.

3. Those who will remain confused, not understanding which side to be on.

Now can you begin to understand we have many good people doing bad things? Small schools are more likely to be filled with virtue, learning, manners and good behavior. satan was successful in wiping out small schools by the myth that large schools are better and are what real schooling is all about. Dr. Stuart states:

> *"Powerful and often compelling myths about real schooling tend to govern our collective assumption about normalcy and these myths have silently, steadfastly advanced the move to larger and more consolidated schools [which have] hampered any real proliferation of small schools model in our country."*[121]

Myths can influence our perception and deceive us because we look to government, and not

God, for our answers. It should not be a surprise that the more we turned towards federal and state dollars to develop our educational programs, the more our schools bowed to the god of government, instead of God, the Creator of all created things. Children have natural attributes of God. They often rebel against today's schools because the very fact of their largeness, gives the souls of children the sense that the schools are less human in nature. Our cure of this system is with facts. Facts with common sense will illuminate why this evil system must go away. We cannot go along with school boards and educational programs which train us for their system, which propagate the bad fruit we now eat, from the "bigger is better" philosophy. It is poisoned fruit. Again, from "The Cost Effectiveness of Small Schools":

> *"Americans are trained by a **culture of consumerism** to think that not only is bigger, better, but that just being 'new' is a virtue."*[122]

"Trained by a culture of consumerism"...this is hitting the nail on the head! Consumerism is under a spirit. Which spirit? Our Lady tells us:

March 25, 1996

> **"...due to the 'spirit of consumerism,' one forgets what it means to love and to cherish true values...Do not let satan attract you through material things but, little children, decide for God who is freedom and love. Choose life and not death of the soul..."**

We do not have true values in our school systems because the purpose of cattle handling facilities is to slaughter; slaughter like cattle at a packing house. Your child is only a number. That is how the system sees them. Yes, good-willed teachers want to help their students, but the systems' infrastructure does not have the ability to allow teachers to do what the heart would like to do. One-room schoolhouses all day, every day, with all students, all year make it possible to develop deep relationships. Youth, today, are forced to be educated in a system built on the spirit of consumerism and therefore, our nation and the world has forgotten **"what it means to love and to cherish true values."** True values of faith and love of God. True values of patriotism and love of country. True values of marriage and family. True values of living in a society that values God, family and country.

Following Our Lady's messages, here at Caritas, we evolved through prayer, to the best infrastructure and system for educating our children—body, mind and soul. In the beginning of our walk with Our Lady, our children were in big schools. We then progressed to better quality Catholic schools. But I realized, through prayer, what good would it do to instill values into our children, only to send them out integrated with other children who were not being taught the same values at home? My children were still being exposed to wrong mentalities and teachings even in "good Catholic schools." We then discovered the richness of homeschooling. But though homeschooling was good, yet still, it was not the best answer. It lacks social contact with other kids throughout the day. Through years of prayer, Our Lady evolved us into a small one-room schoolhouse, which has operated at Caritas for 30 years. This little one-room schoolhouse, with its first through twelfth grade, has graduated 18 students over a quarter of a century, with an average of 10–14 students each year in the classroom. All those who have graduated from our little schoolhouse are thriving in what they do today in life. Because the older children help to teach the younger ones, learning how to deal with children of all different ages, our students have gained a confidence in interacting with people of all different ages.

Larger schools have proven they are not what built America nor will they continue to build America. It was the one-room schoolhouses that built America and will revive it, coupled with repentance and prayer. Susan Blystone writes in "Old School: Reflections of One-room schoolhouse Teachers."

> *"One-room schoolhouses remained the backbone of American education for more than 200 years. By the time of World War II, the era was waning and the little schools were closed as a trend toward* ***consolidation*** *began."* [123]

What resulted from the "consolidation of schools," was the concentration of students in one large building, which caused the wiping out of one-room schoolhouses altogether. The refinement of "cattle-handling" schools began through an approach of efficiency, which has resulted in transforming our children's behavior to fit the ready-made mold that schools require today. A host of other problems ensued from that direction.

Is it possible to break up the cattle handling school systems? Very much so. Illinois State University located in Normal, Illinois, published in their 1935 catalog:

> *"...teachers in Illinois are needed for the 10,000 one room schools."*[124]

One-room schoolhouses were in large numbers across America. One-room schoolhouses are far superior to the present cattle-handling facilities. Our little schoolhouse at Caritas is approximately 30' × 30'. It is a simple structure. Most one-room schoolhouses average this size. The name of our school is *Our Lady of Victory's Little Schoolhouse.* It is one of the diamonds of the Community of Caritas. How did it occur? Our Lady asked for a community to be formed in 1988, during an apparition to Medjugorje visionary, Marija, in the Bedroom of Apparitions, my home at Caritas. Of course, it took time after Our Lady's request to form a community. In the meantime, our family, who hosted Marija, prayed and fasted for Our Lady's intentions. These prayers and sacrifices were a causation which brought about an effect.

It was six years before the Community became something meaningful. Over time, one of the effects, as a result of the causation of prayer and fasting, was the manifestation of our one-room schoolhouse. Do you not think that if you prayed for three hours every day and offered continual sacrifices to be guided by the Holy Spirit that you would be given the inspiration and knowledge that would guide your steps? Our one-room schoolhouse was not planned. It was not a vision; it was revealed. It simply happened over the years. There are no discipline problems, no Ritalin or other drugs to keep our children quiet and docile in their seats, no behavior problems. Our school kids often have knives in their pockets going to school. For them it is a tool. They have brought their bow and arrows and, on occasion, their BB and pellet guns, when outside the window squirrels are eating our pecans off our trees.

There is something of Heaven in Our Lady of Victory's Little Schoolhouse, planted in the middle of the woods, surrounded by cows, a hay barn, rope swings, with *The Tabernacle of Our Lady's Messages* towering above it, and baby calves that they play with on their breaks. The school is only a 30-second walk away. The little school is a beautiful part of Our Lady's plans. Our children walk to school. There is no heat. Heat is provided by a wood-burning stove. Cruelly, by the way the world operates, the children and youth have to cut and split the firewood if they want to stay warm.

They also have to haul the wood to the school. On cold mornings, they crowd around the wood-burning stove. It is not what the country song lyrics say, *"I had it so hard, I had to walk uphill to school both ways."* However, this one-room school-house, in its natural surroundings, tames and consoles the spirit, not Ritalin or antidepressant drugs. Our Lady of Victory's Little Schoolhouse teaches reading, writing and arithmetic. All of which are used immediately in apprenticeship. The children apply the schooling in our carpentry shop, welding shop, pottery shop, and many trades, such as construction, electrical, plumbing, excavation, horticulture, etc., that they are exposed to when they join adult community members in various projects after school and in the summer months. The school itself deals with hyperactivity by getting rid of it in the way we are structured, through our agrarian way of life. This is our therapy. You may think you cannot do this because you live in a subdivision.

Common sense tells you it is wrong to expect children and teenagers to sit still in a seat from 8:00 AM to 3:00 PM, and then hours of homework at home, with a couple of small breaks, even when adults cannot do so. In Scandinavia, it is not uncommon for younger grades to go outside fifteen minutes every hour.[125] God made kids and packed them with youthful energy. When I was in the sixth grade, I had my desk taken away because I could not sit still. The nuns made me sit on the floor for three months. Eventually, I learned to correct my behavior. To drug youth and drain their energy, in order to keep them still, is to turn them into something they are not. In Our Lady of Victory's Little Schoolhouse, when one of the students is rambunctious, it is dealt with naturally. When you have a range of 3% to as much as 40% of a 3,000 student population on Ritalin or other stimulant drugs, it is no wonder the six problems listed about crime, thievery, violence, etc., are found in big schools. Go back to that page (pg. 163) and reread it. Let it be an incentive to change this very evil system. Actually destroy the system of cattle-handling facilities.

Recently, teachers from Colorado and Arkansas went on strike. One of their main issues was the number of students per classroom being too large.

Consider a teacher's dilemma with how to manage 25–33 primary-aged students in one classroom; that is kindergarten, first, second and third graders. Upper grades are no better regarding classroom size on a national average. One teacher was quoted saying she wants no more than 25 students in a classroom so she can give each student more attention. Isn't that interesting? They still buy the lie of the larger schools, while trying to break down the numbers to fix the problem. But if you gave them what they want by busting up the school into individual one-room schoolhouses across the district, dividing the tax money up per schoolhouse, with one teacher, or even two, responsible for a single schoolhouse, they most likely would object. They accept the lie of the large "less human" school, while at the same time want to make within the giant school a bunch of one-room schoolhouse size classrooms of 25 or fewer students! The truth calls out to them in what should be done, but the system is accepted and their inner spirit tells them it's a lie, so they try to band-aid it with smaller classes under one roof of consolidation as if that will solve the problems. It will not. When errors are so rooted, no one will challenge them, mostly because one cannot see them. Turning around the cattle-handling system seems impossible. Our Lady tells us just the opposite. She says, now is the time to turn everything upside down and to turn things around. We have arrived at the point, if one takes action, where action will result in good change, because Heaven is on the side of the one who seeks good. Our Lady said:

June 2, 2017

> **"...be ready. This time is a turning point...I am calling you anew to faith and hope..."**

Meaning, to tear down the school walls, you need faith and hope and then act. The cattle-handling facilities are destined to fall because the system does not glorify God.

How Do We Do It?

First, do not defeat yourself into thinking and saying it can't be done. All across America, in neighborhoods, rural areas, etc., parents can join together and organize a one-room schoolhouse on every couple of blocks. Even in the ghettos, "Big Mama" can rule the roost for a couple of blocks to keep order and safety.* But how? We, at Caritas, did it by deciding to do it. Your 'teacher,' Our Lady, will show you what moves to make and what steps to take. It will manifest through you just doing it. Go through the door and take the next step. If the door remains closed, go to another door. If it stays closed, try another approach. One thing Our Lady taught us, which has become a part of

* A Friend of Medjugorje's family was on the poor side of middle class, but still had a maid come to their home a couple of days a week. He and his other three siblings addressed her as Aunt Maybell and he often spoke fondly of her, saying: "If we didn't respect that 250-pound black mama, she'd slap us little white kids across the room. We didn't mess with Aunt Maybell." A Friend of Medjugorje has spoken about this for decades, that the mayor, police, sheriff, etc., should devise the means for appointing or electing a "Big Mama" from every neighborhood and set rules, like curfew, no drugs, no graffiti, keeping yards orderly, starting one-room schoolhouses, etc. One Aunt Maybell, appointed by a sheriff, who can deputize would bring back law and order to crime infested communities, get rid of troublemakers and provide a better future to inner-city children and youth. The deputized Maybells only have to turn in the bad apples.

the heart and foundation of our mission, is to work to achieve whatever God points out for us to do. We do it through the following method:

1. Prayer
2. Approach
3. Patience

From the top of the mission of Caritas, this is how Our Lady works with us. Some things took years to achieve, even more than a couple of decades. Some of the things we have prayed for have yet to happen but we have hope and faith to continue praying. We never stop praying, approaching the obstacles and having patience for Heaven to align everything for us. God aligns everything. Sometimes it can take a long time, because the Heavenly Father will not violate man's free will to make something happen when man's will is blocking it. God can, however, create circumstances to move man towards coming into alignment with His Will, but He still expects you to be active and moving towards His goals for you. You will learn by what you are doing. The task, itself, will teach you whether or not it will work. If it doesn't work, it teaches you to come up with a different plan or strategy. Either way you learn and move forward. Do not be daunted; just keep moving. We, at Caritas, never stop pursuing what we set out to achieve. We may have to change our approach or tactic, but we never give up because we, as well as you, are to change your own future and by that means, will change the world's future as well. Our Lady said:

June 15, 2012

"...set out into the future..."

Break'em up. Begin a revolution.

Mr. Educator, Tear Down These Walls!

"God ordained man, for each one, to be connected to the agrarian life. While there are many occupations, only one was ordained by God. God speaks to mankind in the Garden of Eden after Adam sinned:

> ***'Cursed is the ground because of you! In toil you shall eat its yield all the days of your life. Thorns and thistles it shall bear for you, and you shall eat the grass of the field. By the sweat of your brow you shall eat bread, until you return to the ground from which you were taken.'***
> Genesis 3:19

Because of the rapid deterioration of the world, I have repeatedly said, regarding the coming devestating economic crash forcing man back to the soil, 'Get your food from your ground to your mouth as quickly as possible.' You still have the ability to establish your food chain in the greenwood, whereas you won't in the drywood when you will have an abundant harvest of thorns and thistles to scratch your food from the soil. Every man, despite his work, must be involved in the agrarian life. Thereby, the children will be raised around and engaged with the agrarian life which is exposed to nature, instead of being disengaged from nature, as the youth are raised today.

Friend of Medjugorje

CHAPTER TWELVE

Healing Nature's Way

As early as July 1982, Our Lady began speaking about fasting in Her messages in Medjugorje. She began asking the visionaries and the parish to fast twice a week, every Wednesday and Friday. She defined what the best fast was—a 24-hour period, in which one eats only bread and drinks only water, beginning when one wakes in the morning until the following morning. She spoke about the spiritual benefits that come from fasting and that fasting can even stop wars and suspend the laws of nature.

July 21, 1982

> **"The best fast is on bread and water. Through fasting and prayer, one can stop wars, one can suspend the laws of**

nature. Charity cannot replace fasting. Those who are not able to fast can sometime replace it with prayer, charity, and a Confession; but everyone, except the sick, must fast."

Our Lady was clear. 'No one' should excuse themselves from fasting, except the sick. Taking Our Lady at Her word, Medjugorje believers around the world began to fast just as Our Lady said. When I founded the Community of Caritas in 1988, fasting twice a week on bread and water became part of our way of life. We live a very rigorous life—physically, mentally and spiritually demanding—yet Our Lady gave no excuse except for the sick. She even led us to do nine-day fasts on bread and water. We never lessened our schedule of work and prayer during the nine-day fast. Many times we were in the middle of projects that kept us up until the wee hours of the night, and up again for 5 AM prayer—making the fast more difficult, but the spiritual, and even physical, benefits we experienced gave us cognition that fasting is "a good" for us. We were not looking for confirmation; our faith in Our Lady's instructions was complete. However, our faith in Her was rewarded by the experience of the good fasting brought to us.

Anything good for man will be eventually opposed by darkness. And fasting began to be spoken about, written about, reported on and denounced by news organizations around the world. Doctors and scientists were weighing in with their opinions of how dangerous fasting is and those who are promoting it should not be listened to. People began contacting Caritas to express concern about fasting. We were not swayed against fasting, first because Our Lady would never ask us to do something that was bad for us. Secondly, because we had found fasting to be beneficial both spiritually and physically.

Our Lady did not specifically speak of the physical benefits of fasting for our physical health but having faith in Our Lady made us believe those benefits existed, regardless of what the latest science fads were reporting. In time, truth wins out. Eventually, science began to validate the good that "intermittent fasting" does for the human body. Also, specific data shows that **fasting twice a week** helps to flush out poisonous toxins that build up in the body, leading to a physical rejuvenation of the body, among other benefits, that help in the process of rest and healing. Those who are searching for a healthier lifestyle are often led to intermittent fasting.

God the Creator made the human body and programmed within it what will keep the body healthy and functioning properly. The processed foods we eat are filled with poison, and the attitude of many is that they *"live to eat rather than eat to live,"* resulting in overindulgence and obesity. As the saying goes, "You are what you eat," and the intake of foods that the body cannot process is killing people through disease and toxic chemicals, affecting people not only physically, but mentally as well. Our Lady is communicating a great deal when She says:

February 2, 2014

> **"...I desire that by fasting and prayer you obtain from the Heavenly Father the cognition of what is natural and holy – Divine..."**

The natural and the holy will bring the Divine, the alignment of Heaven with the physical—the spiritual realm connecting to the physical realm. Harmony is the result and healing then is possible. It is not only in fasting that this is found, but there are many truths hidden in Our Lady's messages regarding all aspects of life that will lead to wholeness and healing when we align our lives with the guidance Our Lady is giving.

A Remedy Right Under Our Noses: What Nature Gives to Man

Our world is a highly stressful place to live. We live in an antichrist system which purposely and thoughtfully has been built for the destruction of man. God created man to be able to handle a great number of challenges, and also the way to heal, but today, satan manages to keep man in an uninterrupted state of stress and crisis that weakens all levels of being: spiritual, mental, physical and emotional. Florence Williams, author of the 2017 best-selling book, The Nature Fix: Why Nature Makes Us Happier, Healthier, and More Creative, states:

> *"The demands and constant stimuli of modern life tend to trigger our sympathetic nervous system, which governs fight-or-flight behaviors. And trigger it and trigger it. We suffer the consequences: a long trail of research dating back to the 1930s shows people who produce chronically high cortisol levels and high blood pressure are more prone to heart disease, metabolic disease, dementia and depression. More recent research shows that the steady stress of urban living changes the brain in ways that can*

increase our odds of schizophrenia, anxiety and mood disorders." [126]

It is important to know what cortisol is and its importance in the regulation of our bodies. Cortisol is nature's built-in alarm system. It is responsible for regulating how much sugar (glucose) and fat gets stored in your body, and how much is released to use for fuel. It's also your body's main stress hormone. When you are stressed, your adrenal glands release a burst of cortisol to help you cope, temporarily increasing your blood sugar for a boost of energy.

In addition, cortisol also:

- Controls blood sugar levels in the body
- Regulates metabolism
- Keeps inflammation down
- Contributes to memory formation
- Regulates the body's salt and water balance
- Affects blood pressure

Cortisol can effect almost every organ system in your body. When your body is in high alert, through stress or crisis, your body produces higher levels of cortisol that can temporarily shut down certain body functions that are being affected by the stress or crisis situation, such as your digestive system, your immune system, or even your growth processes. Once the pressure, crisis or danger passes, your cortisol goes to work to calm you down by bringing your heart, blood pressure and other body systems back to normal. This is how your body naturally deals with the normal stress and pressures of life.

However, today, millions of people are under constant and extreme stress. This is when your body begins to produce **too much cortisol** and it can cause negative and dangerous reactions in your body. When the body is in a constant state of pressure or stress, cortisol levels can cause the body's systems to begin to dysfunction and health problems begin to surface such as:

- Anxiety and depression
- Headaches

- Heart disease
- Memory and concentration problems
- Problems with digestion
- Trouble sleeping
- Weight gain, among many other symptoms

What is often offered as a remedy for these health issues? Antidepressants, sleeping pills, diuretics, or laxatives for rapid weight loss, etc. These 'do not' fix the problem; they mask the problem and create new problems that compound the difficulties a person is experiencing. This is the state of the average modern man today. This is the state of almost all mankind. It is unsustainable and we are seeing the results—a total spiraling out of control of our culture as is evident in the destruction of the health of people worldwide in countless ways.

William Butler Yeats, in his prophetic 1919 poem, "The Second Coming," captures the dark time in which we are living:

*Turning and turning in the widening gyre**
The falcon cannot hear the falconer;
***Things fall apart**; the centre cannot hold;*
Mere anarchy is loosed upon the world,
The blood-dimmed tide is loosed, and everywhere
The ceremony of innocence is drowned;
The best lack all conviction, while the worst
Are full of passionate intensity.

What does the line "The falcon cannot hear the falconer" mean? One commentator had great insight into this passage when he wrote:

"Falcon is a type of domesticated bird and the person who tames it is called a falconer. And this process is called falconry. Every falcon obeys the rule of his master who trained them. They have good connections and can easily understand each other. The bird is not supposed to keep flying in circles forever because they have to come back and land on the falconer's glove.

* A spiral or vortex.

"But W.B. Yeats said that the falcon cannot hear the falconer. And it has a deep symbolic meaning. He wanted to say that the human (falcon) doesn't obey their Creator (falconer). They are moving away from the path shown by their Creator. People only do hypocrisy, do politics of lies, people kill, people commit heresy in the name of religion. Science has shaken their faith in God and they compare God with science. So, they lose their spiritual value. They create war with themselves which is against God's command. For their pleasure, they invoke vulgar things into their culture. In the greed for power, they do not hesitate to take people's lives. They are destroying their culture, their religion, their nature, even their morality.

"This is the complete opposite of the path shown by the Creator. It is as if people are following the path shown by inhumans. It seems

> *that there is no Creator in this civilization. Yeats wants to say these things within a single line with the symbolic way.”*[127]

God has His ways of leading man back to His truths and while nations grapple with the destruction of their people, they have stumbled upon a remedy that man cannot replicate as it is sourced in God, the Creator Himself. It should come as no surprise that this same remedy is confirmed in Our Lady’s messages many times over. In fact, Our Lady offers the ultimate remedy that truly brings healing: go into nature and learn from it what prayer can do for your body and soul. Don’t just read what follows, instead hear what is being said:

January 27, 1986

> **“Every second of prayer is like a drop of dew in the morning which refreshes fully each flower, each blade of grass and the earth. In the same way prayer re-**

> **freshes man. When man is tired, he gets rest. When he is troubled, he finds peace again. Man renews himself and can, once again, listen to the words of God.**
>
> **"How the scenery is beautiful when we look at nature in the morning in all its freshness! But more beautiful, much more, is it when we look at a man who brings to others peace, love, and happiness. Children, if you could know what prayer brings to man! Especially personal prayer. Man can thus become a really fresh flower for God. You see how drops of dew stay long on flowers until the first rays of sun come."**

But wait! Our Lady says it is "prayer" which brings healing, not nature. Really? Read it more closely with prayer and you will see that nature leads to contemplation and prayer which leads to the fruit Our Lady speaks of, "peace, love and happiness."

Our Lady has spoken about nature often and offers it as a key that will open the door of your heart to healing in a way that man cannot find on his own.

April 25, 1993

> **"...I invite you all to awaken your hearts to love. Go into nature and look how nature is awakening and it will be a help for you to open your hearts to the love of God the Creator..."**

September 25, 2012

> **"...When in nature you look at the richness of the colors which the Most High gives to you, open your heart and pray with gratitude for all the good that you have and say: 'I am here created for eternity'—and yearn for heavenly things because God loves you with immeasurable love..."**

February 25, 2010

> **"...this time of grace, when nature also prepares to give the most beautiful colors of the year, I call you, little children, to open your hearts to God the Creator for Him to transform and mold you in His image, so that all the good which has fallen asleep in your hearts may awaken to a new life and a longing towards eternity..."**

God speaks to you personally in nature. God has always been. Therefore, when nature came into being, it came out of the very being of God Himself. Where else would it come from? He created it and everything that it is. That's why nature speaks to you. We are not talking about a 'new age' worship that is of satan, who mimics God. God, through nature, will communicate to you and help to heal your difficulties and console you. How do we know

God will speak to you? Because Our Lady said on March 25, 1990:

> **"...God...sends you messages through men, '*__nature__*' and so many things which can only help you to *understand* that you 'must' change the direction of your life..."**

The world is changing. The timing of Our Lady's appearance in Medjugorje in 1981, was calculated by Heaven to put Her out in front of so many diabolical changes in the world. God sent Her to alert those who would see and listen to the signs, signs that were given by God to help man change the direction of his life, to be the seeds that will bring in a Way of Life in a New Time, a time that man will return to the soil, an agrarian life. Those who do not change the direction of their lives away from where the world is going will be forced into the agrarian life, whether or not they want it. But, because most of the world's population ignored the signs that God has repeatedly given, God will renew and repronounce the sentence He gave to Adam in the Garden of Eden, for all generations. The Second Eve, Mary, Our Lady, is here, heralding that we have separated ourselves from the soil (agrarian, nature, etc.). Therefore, this modern world **will** be going back to it.

In the verse from Genesis that was quoted at the beginning of this chapter, this sentence of God is rapidly descending upon man now, in our time. For those who have not used these 40 years — 1981 to 2022 — preparing to go back to the soil, while in the "greenwood," it will be bitter for you once we enter into the period of the "drywood." When everything falls apart, how do you get back to the soil? You get back by hunger and buckets of sweat from your brow. All the above is stated to show that the world is sick and nature, with God's grace, gives the medicine. You can choose life or death. Our Lady said on March 25, 2019:

> **"…'<u>In</u>' nature seek God who created you, because nature speaks and fights for life and not for death…"**

The signs scream out to man — the path the world is on will lead to death. Our Lady of Medjugorje, in Her apparitions, told visionary, Marija, to tell the whole world that the cure for man and the world, is to wake up before it is too late for you.

January 25, 2021

> **"…This is a time of awakening and of giving birth. As nature which gives itself, you also, little children, ponder how much you have received. Be joyful bearers of peace and love <u>that it may be good for you on earth</u>…"**

Man can take a joyful path that will "be good" for him or stay on the bad path that won't be good for him. Our Lady is here to reveal how to change a negative to a positive.

And again, Our Lady speaks of nature and prayer:

Follow up to January 27, 1986, message:

> **"Nature, in this way, is renewed and refreshed. For the beauty of nature, a daily renewal and refreshment is necessary. Prayer refreshes man in the same way, to renew him and give him strength…"**

What the Research Shows:

There is great interest in studying the effects of man being in nature today—all because of the devastating effects the technological world is having on people. Clinical depression, mental health issues, the deterioration of the physical health and wellbeing in people, rampant suicides, etc., all have risen to astronomical heights coinciding with the rise of technologies used by the common man everyday. The deterioration of the mental and physical health of man then leads to the rise of scientific research as man grapples with these issues. And where does the research lead? It seems that all roads lead back to God's Creation and the world of nature. Florence Williams', The Nature Fix, documents the most recent and cutting edge research of the healing power within nature for man. Her book was fascinating and eye-opening giving the scientific data that confirms Our Lady's direction for man. For those who would like to delve more deeply into the subject, Williams' book is a good place to start.

Take for instance, South Korea, who has earned the distinction of being the most wired country in the world. This means ninety percent of homes have the fastest download speeds in the world. Video games have created "gaming addictions" in 8% of Koreans under the age of 40 and for kids between the ages of nine and twelve, it increases to 14%. Just this one statistic is responsible for reeking havoc in the lives of youth. Desperate for solutions, they began studying the effects of nature on their own people. Two South Korean studies looked at 11 and 12 year olds who were borderline technology addicts. After trips to the forest for two days each, researchers found both lowered cortisol levels and significant improvements in measures of self-esteem, and the benefits lasted for two weeks. Time in the forest also led them to report feeling happier, less anxious and more optimistic about their futures.[128]

Another example has to do with **natural killer cells, called NK cells.** These specialized cells protect us from disease agents and can, like cortisol, be reliably measured in a laboratory. NK cells send messages to tumors and virus-infected cells to annihilate them. Factors like stress, aging and pesticides can reduce your NK count. A study in Japan wanted to know if nature could increase your NK cells and thereby help you fight infections and cancer. In the first control group, Tokyo businessmen on three consecutive mornings went on a two-hour hike in nature. The second control group of businessmen took a two-hour walk in an urban area on three consecutive days. At the end of the third day, blood tests in control group one showed their NK killer cells had increased by 40%. The boost lasted seven days. A month later, their NK cell count was still 15% higher than when they started. In contrast, the study showed with the businessmen who walked the same amount of time in the city that their NK cell levels **did not change**. The researchers believe the boost in NK cells in the first control group came from aromas from trees, among other things.[129]

From this and many other studies that measured the wellness of individuals after being in nature consistently, Japan's government began creating "Forest Therapy Trails." They coined a phrased, "forest baths" which means to let nature into your body through all five senses. Japan's government has funded $4,000,000 in forest-bathing research since 2003.[130] The entire nation is encouraged to commit to a certain amount of hours each month to be in nature. Many businesses require their employees to do so. They made these radical moves because Japan, being a highly technological culture, has the third highest suicide rate in the world. One-fifth of Japan's residents live in Tokyo, with 8.7 million who ride the metro every day. Going back to nature has been revolutionary for the Japanese in terms of an increase in wellness for their people.

It is not only Japan, but many nations are taking note of this research and doing their own, coming up with the same conclusions: that *"peaceful or nurturing elements of nature helped us regain equanimity, cognitive clarity, empathy and hope."*[131] One study showed a 50% improvement in creativity after just a few days in nature. Dr. David Strayer, a cognitive psychologist at the University of Utah, stated about nature experience:

> *"I think there's a recalibration of your senses, of seeing and noticing."*[132]

One of the participants in a study that Strayer organized, Paul Atchley, had this question:

> *"Is the explosion of attractive technologies that give our brains social interactions negatively impacting us, and is the cure to go back to an environment that our brain resonates with? Tech is leading us in a negative direction and nature may prevent that."*[133]

As you have read earlier, Our Lady often speaks about nature as if it should be a common experience of man to be in nature, yet how many of us have our eyes, ears, minds, and hearts opened to the changing landscape that nature provides for us on a daily basis? It is to our detriment that we do not.

February 25, 2020

> **"… You are so flooded by earthly concerns, you do not even feel that spring is at the threshold…As '<u>nature fights in silence</u>' for new life, also you are called**

to open yourselves in prayer to God, in Whom you will find peace and warmth of the spring sun in your hearts..."

Ruth Ann Atchley, a psychologist from the University of Kansas, stated:

> *"My hypothesis is when you're engaged in nature, it leads to mindfulness. It's passive, the world is coming and going. It's so good for depression. When you walk out in nature, it's like wearing rose-colored glasses. In nature everything is a little more positive, there's a little more connectedness. This is the world in which we are supposed to be."*[134]

Again, through the world's love affair with technology, we chain our minds, our eyes, our ears to e-mails, alerts and sounds. It is difficult to filter through so much stimulus coming at us at all times, and give our full attention to that which is meaningful to get our tasks done and to think deeply, which is necessary to our well-being as spiritual beings. Paul Atchley states:

> *"Attention is everything...Without it, we don't see, hear, taste. Your brain keeps track of about four things at once...Most of what the brain is doing is filtering, tuning stuff out so we can focus in on things that are relevant."*[135]

Our Lady also emphasizes the importance of being attentive.

February 21, 1982

> **"...I will make you attentive. I will guide you on a sure way."**

January 28, 1987

> **"...Whenever I come to you my Son comes with me, but so does satan. You permitted, without noticing, his influences on you and he drives you on. Sometimes you understand that some-**

> **thing you have done is not agreeable to God, but quickly you no longer pay attention to it…"**

September 9, 1988

> **"…your Mother is warning that satan is at work. I would like you to pay special attention to the fact that satan is at work in a special way with the young…"**

February 2, 2009

> **"Dear children! With a Motherly Heart, today I desire to remind you of, mainly to draw your attention to…"**

Our Lady is drawing you to see that the world's problem is a lack of clear discernment. So much of the world is walking in falsehood, fostered by the king of darkness. Man must reflect and think how we have been living lies.

Atchley speaks of the importance of attention when in nature and how it lends itself to move man to think on a higher plane, which confirms Our Lady's words in how we can have an encounter with God in nature.

Regarding the positive results being observed among the test group, Paul Atchley states:

> *"What this environment is doing to us right now is giving us fewer choices. And by having fewer choices, your attentional system functions better for higher order things. In the office environment, you've got emails, alerts, sounds. That's a lot of filtering and so it's harder to think deeply. Here the filtering requirements are not demanding so you have the capacity to focus on deeper thoughts."*[136]

Florence Williams is led into a deeper understanding of what is taking place in the human psyche among nature's beauty and raises an important point:

> *"Humans have brains that are sensitive to social and emotional stress and we always*

have. Perhaps what matters is not the source of the stress but the ability to recover from it. This is a key point, because it's perhaps what we've lost by giving up our connection to the night skies, the bracing air and the companionate chorus of birds. When I'm walking across a pleasant landscape, I feel I have time and I feel I have space. I'm breathing deeply things that smell good and seeing things that bring delight. It's hard not to feel the pull of a grounded reality when you're dipping into a muddy trail or a flowing river."[137]

A Nature Bath: How Nature Impacts Our Senses

Sense of Smell:

Odor hits the brain's emotional neurons more powerfully than other senses. The human nose can detect one trillion odors. Only recently scientists are discovering that the nose leads to a direct pathway to the brain. Pollution particles inhaled impact the brain. Heavy traffic highways, school parking lots, highly industrialized zones in cities, etc., provide high levels of exhaust fumes that are carried through molecules into our nasal receptors and the closer you are to these areas, the higher the risk of autism, stroke and cognitive decline in aging. If such negative results happen through breathing in poisons, what will be the result of breathing in "good" molecules through nature?

Florence Williams reports that one study in 2011 to measure how much pollution is removed by trees in the United States estimated the number to be 17.4 million tons of air pollution per year. Everyone has experienced that when breathing in the fresh air and aromas of a forest or seaside, makes one feel better. It is not only getting away from polluted areas but nature actually removes air pollution, whereby leaves and soil soak up polluted particles. Pollution is known to even cause diseases, so scientists believe it is essential for health and well-being to not only remove oneself from polluted areas, but to submerge oneself into nature which will bring renewal.[138]

Sense of Hearing:

Noise pollution can negatively affect the brain and its functioning as well. Even noises that you don't necessarily notice influence not only how your brain responds but also can elevate your heart rate, blood pressure and respiration. Environmental noise can cause hypertension if the decibels are loud enough. Natural sound, on the other hand, can bring healing. Joshua Smyth, a biobehavioral health psychologist says:

> *"We should think about soundscapes as medicine…It's like a pill. You can prescribe sounds or a walk in the park in much the way we prescribe exercise. Do it twenty minutes a day as a lifetime approach, or you can do it*

as an acute stress intervention. When you're stressed, go to a quiet place."[139]

Recall the message of February 25, 2020. Our Lady said:

"…Nature fights in silence for new life…"

There is a reason that Dr. Smyth calls soundscapes "medicine…it's like a pill." Pharmaceutical companies have sold the world on all we need is the right pill to take away all of our problems and difficulties. This is diabolical thinking. God programmed into nature what is necessary to bring peace to man's spirit. And while being in nature may not bring man to full healing and other measures may need to be taken, being in nature will always be a positive for man and will improve his condition for a more holistic outcome in his overall health.

Amazingly, science has been able to narrow down the three nature sounds that have the greatest impact on bringing a sense of peace and mental calmness: wind, water and birds. In particular, studies using birdsong consistently show improvements in mood and mental alertness.[140] Just hearing birds singing in the morning or during the day creates a sense of wellness in those who hear it. The sound of rain and rushing waters also soothes the body that is filled with anxiety, leading to calm and peace. And as for the wind, Our Lady gives Her answer:

February 15, 1984

> **"The wind is my sign. I will come in the wind. When the wind blows, know that I am with you…"**

Sense of Sight:

A study in a Michigan prison in 1981 showed that when prison cells faced rolling farmland and trees, in contrast to a barren courtyard on the other side of the facility, there were fewer sick call visits overall from prisoners facing a green view. In a similar study in a hospital, those in rooms with a "green" view needed fewer postoperative days in the hospital, requested less pain medication and were described in nurses' notes as having better attitudes.

In similar studies in office buildings and schools: nature views increased worker productivity, less job stress, higher academic grades and test scores and less aggression in inner-city residents. Studies have linked asphalt views to a greater tendency for aggressive and violent behaviors, and the opposite with nature views. Analyzing 98 buildings over two years, researchers found a striking correlation between the level of greenery around the buildings and the number of assaults, homicides, vehicle thefts, burglary, and arson. Buildings with the greenest views saw 48% fewer property crimes and 56% fewer violent crimes than buildings with the least greenery.

Another amazing discovery regarding how what we see in nature immediately impacts our stress and feelings of well-being is that nature is made up of "fractal dimensions"—patterns that repeat themselves over and over—to infinity. Examples would be the motion of waves of the ocean, or the patterns that trees and branches make in forests and woods crisscrossing each other. When these "fractal dimensions" are viewed in nature (and also in art), the frontal lobes of humans begin to produce, as Williams states, "Those elusive and prized alpha brain waves of a wakefully relaxed state." [141] This occurs even when seen for only one minute when gazing at a picture.

In scientific tests on the Medjugorje visionaries, their brain waves were measured before, during and after they see the Virgin Mary, also known as the moment of "ecstasy." Amazing to the scientists is that in normal humans, unless one has been practicing meditation for years, it is nearly impossible to suddenly enter into the alpha wave state. Yet, the Medjugorje visionaries, as soon as they go into ecstasy, immediately reach the alpha wave state, as if someone turned on a switch, which is contrary to how alpha waves work normally. They are associated with those who reach a very high level of prayer or meditative states, such as what you would find with cloistered monks and nuns, which does not happen instantaneously. Yet, incredibly, God programmed into nature itself what is necessary to bring one into a peaceful, prayerful state of mind. Nature acts upon the physical body the same way prayer and meditation does. But this is what Our Lady has been saying for years:

July 25, 2001

> **"...Make good use of the time of rest and give your soul and your eyes rest in God. Find peace in nature and you will discover God the Creator Whom you will be able to give thanks to for all creatures; then you will find joy in your heart..."**

The brain reacts to these fractal dimensions in such a way that the spirit of man opens to the Creator God. It is an amazing discovery through Our

Lady's messages. Understanding this, one can see easily what is lost in modern architecture. Buildings are ugly as sin today. They all look the same, with no individuality, no creativity, no beauty, no mystery. Contemporary leads away from God's beauty. Contemporary is man's beauty which is dull, cold and lifeless. Having traveled overseas well over 200 times, gives one an education by studying and observing incredible architecture. Having the real experience of looking at centuries-old renaissance buildings was an apprenticeship in learning what beauty is and how prayer inspires architectural masterpieces.

Not following modernism's direction and being in landscaping and excavating, greatly influenced the architectural development of Caritas of Birmingham. For example, the Mother House of Caritas' operations, *The Tabernacle of Our Lady's Messages,* is beautifully designed and gives pleasant feelings. It is laid out in its natural topography, just as it was before the building was built. In the modern architectural world, excavators and bulldozers destroy topography. These machines should be used as a paintbrush, not as wrecking balls. Most of the designs of homes, commercial buildings, etc., in urban environments are void of these fractal dimensions, and instead are made up of parallel, perpendicular lines and similar geometric designs. Summarizing physicist Richard Taylor's research, Williams' states that, *"we need these natural patterns to look at, and we're not getting enough of them. As we increasingly surround ourselves with straight Euclidean built environments, we risk losing our connection to the natural stress-reducer that is visual fluency."* [142]

How much nature does one need to maintain health in body, mind and spirit? The consensus that developed through many different studies is that the more nature exposure, the better one feels, which includes stronger positive emotions and lower negative emotions, feeling more creative and feeling psychologically restored. But to be more specific, the biggest boosts occurred after five hours a month in natural settings. If one can go for ten hours a month, which requires about 30 minutes in nature five days a week or two to three days per month, they will reach a new level of wellness. In a study in which 9,000 people were challenged to walk 30 minutes a day in nature for 30 days in a row, only 2,500 people stuck it out, while the vast majority dropped out, unable to build the discipline needed to make a new habit that could transform their physical and emotional well-being. The results of the study:

> *"The more time participants spent in nature, the greater well-being they reported. They seemed to like being in nature so much, they doubled their weekly green time by the end of the month, from five hours to 10. As the month progressed, they also reduced their time in vehicles, texting and e-mailing. They*

reported significant increases in all measures of well-being, including in mood and mental calm, and also decreases in stress and negativity. They slept better and also reported feeling slightly more connected to nature."[143]

How immediate are the positive effects of nature? In just seeing images of nature, subjects reacted positively within 200 milliseconds. One study showed to lower one's blood pressure or cortisol levels and improve mood it took about 15–20 minutes walking in nature. At 45–50 minutes, many people show stronger cognitive performance, feelings of vitality, improved mood, more creativity and overall refreshed.[144]

What else affects nature's ability to restore individuals? Being alone in nature can be more restorative, especially for those who are mentally fatigued or socially stressed. One must also be unplugged from all electronics to see positive results and should try and free their thoughts to emerge themselves more completely in all that nature provides—sights, sounds, smells, touch.

Mental healing comes through nature. Johan Ottosson was hit by a car in Sweden and landed on his head. He spent six months struggling to regain basic skills and fell into a deep depression. What pulled Ottosson out of despair was the land and sea nearby. He became convinced that nature had helped him heal. After studying this subject in school, Ottosson wrote:

> *"Over recent decades we have come from dwelling in another world in which the living worlds of nature either predominated or were near at hand, to dwelling in an environment dominated by a technology which is wondrously powerful and yet nonetheless dead."*[145]

He has been distressed to see that the modern medical establishment has largely forgotten the insights of nature-based healing. He said:

> *"When you built a hospital 100 years ago, you built it around a nice park. That was self-evident. But after about 1930 or 1940, man is treated like a machine. He gets energy and medicine and that's all. We are just now starting to get fuller knowledge back."*[146]

Studies that involve those who have Post-Traumatic Stress Disorder (PTSD) or who have experienced severe trauma also achieve restoration through nature. English poet, William Wordsworth, was a child of trauma. His mother died when he was eight and his father when he was 13. He was separated from his siblings and forced to live with relatives who were cold and indifferent to him. Wordsworth placed a financial strain on the family adding to the stress of the situation. The fact that this happened during the height of his emotional and psychological development only compounded the intensity of his isolation and rejection. Nature became for him a place of comfort and healing and he would return to this central theme over and over again in his writings. Quoting Yale scholar, Geoffry Hartman, Florence Williams elaborated on the value Wordsworth found in nature as a way to handle and heal from the trauma of losing his parents at such a young age.

> *"Nature does everything to prepare you, to make you immune, or to gentle the shock. [Wordsworth] doesn't say there is no shock, or surprise, but that nature aims at a growth of the mind which can absorb or overcome shock."* [147]

The subject of the healing that can be found in nature is fascinating to study, but what is more deeply edifying is that the wisdom found in Our Lady's messages is confirmed once again through the science of our times and that is that God, His peace and His healing are waiting to be rediscovered in His Creation, given to us for that very purpose.

"'Neurologically, [man has not] *caught up with today's overstimulating environment...Getting kids out in nature can make a difference."*[148]

Richard Louv
Author of *Last Child in the Woods*

CHAPTER THIRTEEN

A Remedy for Our Wounded and Restless Hearts

ADHD showed up the same time that schooling became compulsory for all children as the world moved towards industrialization and away from an agrarian way of life. What was normal behavior for children for millennia, especially for boys, slowly became considered disordered behavior, behavior that must be controlled by drugs. When boys were taken from the great outdoors, and their world began to shrink into a 900 square foot classroom that they share with 20–30 other kids, sitting at a desk 4½ to 7 hours a day, with 2–3 hours of homework each night, when even play and sports became highly structured, and screen time on social media or television began filling up the rest of free time, it shouldn't be a wonder why so many children today fit in the "lie-label": "dysfunctional." What should make people wonder is how man accepted such a world for their children to grow up in.

Imagine a group of social "scientists" and government officials making a plan a century ago that would produce monumental changes in the way man lives. Industries were making life easier, more pleasant and with more conveniences for everyone through their creations and inventions. As I wrote nearly 30 years ago in my book I See Far,* the invention of air conditioning and television drew families off of their front porches and into their homes, watching life in front of their black box instead of living life together.

To make the transition into this brave new world, it must start with our children. That is where the change must begin. But there was one catch.

* I See Far was written by a Friend of Medjugorje in 1994. See the order form in the back of the book. Or contact Caritas of Birmingham to order by phone 205-672-2000, on their website Mej.com or through Amazon.com

There would be children who would not be able to adhere or adapt to these changes. For this new system to succeed, the children who wouldn't quite get with the program would have to be medicated so that they would be able to keep aligned with the rest of the children. High energy children who are expected to sit in their seats for hours a day will be bored. They are going to exhibit impulsive behavior that will disrupt class. It is normal to be distracted when bored. But the world wants to restrain them through specially designed drugs that dope them down to calm down their behaviors. Go to the zoo and watch the tigers walk back and forth, back and forth, back and forth the same walk day after day. Many say it is cruel for these animals. Then how much more for kids? Kids are not animals.

Classrooms need a baseline behavior that all students must be held. The nail that sticks up must be hammered down. But since it is for the good of the plan, it should be a sacrifice parents and their children should be willing to make. Right? Today it is estimated that **13.6%** of all teenagers are labeled as a defect and branded with a concocted ailment, ADHD, just because of the gift of energy, which in later life can be an asset in their work. That is a lot of nails to hammer down! In effect, this is how ADHD came to be. It is a manufactured useful social disorder (money) that has found a way to pound a square peg into a round hole. One cannot do that without shattering the peg. The analogy is not too far off the mark, as there are an inestimable number of shattered lives as a result of being "labeled" ADHD. Our Lady said:

January 25, 1997

> **"...You are creating a new world without God, only with your own strength and that is why you are unsatisfied and without joy in the heart..."**

It is interesting that Our Lady gave the above message in 1997, as ADHD cases began to climb significantly in the 1990s. Our Lady reveals the reason for the rise in labeling kids with ADHD. She simply says, **"...You are creating a new world without God..."** Children are not the problem. It is not their genetics. It is not their biology. The problem is that man has created a world that requires children to be medicated in order for them to be able to function within that world. When one tries to fix the child, rather than the environment that does not allow him to thrive—as with every misdiagnosis, it leads to greater problems and difficulties, even to tragedies. But there is hope if the right diagnosis can be made.

In the book, The Nature Fix, introduced in the last chapter, author Florence Williams followed the life of a middle schooler from Connecticut by the name of Zack Smith, labeled with ADHD by the time he was in the second grade. Exhibiting all the classic symptoms—hyperactivity, impulsivity and distractibility—his parents dutifully filled prescription after prescription, year after year, to keep a handle on his behavior. Many of the drugs didn't work. His ability to control his anger (which the medication fostered) became a concern that led to suspension from school. He was an unhappy kid who lost all desire and motivation to be in school. His parents, deeply concerned with what the future held for their son, made a radical move and took him out of school in his eighth grade year. Zack ended up in North Carolina, at a camp specifically established for kids with the stigma of ADHD and other learning disabilities.

Named SOAR, the camp/boarding school was founded in 1977 by Jonathan Jones who had grown up with so-called learning disabilities and believed he had something better to offer youth labeled with the scam called, ADHD. He believed that focusing on an individual's strengths, rather than their deficits, was critical to a child's success in school and in life. It shouldn't take a brain surgeon to figure that out, but living in a world where common sense has all but been lost, Jones stands out from the crowd. Jones also believed that kids labeled with ADHD would flourish in natural surroundings, so much so that he made this a core principle of SOAR.

Most of the youth who enroll in SOAR's program do not typically have that much contact with the outdoor world, let alone three-week long adventures in horseback riding, canoeing, rock climbing, backpacking, etc. So distant are some kids from being in nature that the very thought of it fills them with anxiety. But slowly, being emersed in the natural world, a conversion happens, even a transformation. Florence Williams wrote of Zack's transformation after his first nature excursion in Wyoming:

"Something clicked under the wide Wyoming skies. He found he was able to focus on tasks;

> *he was making friends and feeling less terrible about himself.* ***Zack turned his restlessness into a craving for adventure—which is perhaps what it was meant to be all along.***"[149]

While it is not a specific goal of SOAR to get kids off their medications, it can lead to that and often does. It did with Zack. His parents began the process of getting him off his anxiety medications, while slowly lessening the doses of whatever stimulant he was taking. **It is important to note that this should always be done under a doctor's supervision.** Zack's mother exclaimed, "*The changes in him have been nothing short of miraculous. Now he's just happy.*" [150] SOAR's approach is to look to the needs of the whole child and change the environment to make the child successful. When they do that, the child finds healing, success, and happiness, which leads to what conclusion? It wasn't the child that needed fixing. This comes from SOAR's website:

"With the goal of success in mind, our programs provide challenges that build self-esteem, self-confidence, and self-reliance. Each participant is challenged in a variety of adventure activities (backpacking, rock climbing, canoeing, among others), and pushed beyond their comfort zone with support and encouragement. These experiences empower the participant to make healthy choices, learn more about themselves, overcome challenges, and relate lessons learned from these experiences to other aspects of their lives."[151]

What does that sound like? It sounds like the world that God created it to be—not what it has turned out to be. Unfortunately, only 32 children are accepted into SOAR's program each year with a cost of $61,000 per child, and additional costs on top of that. SOAR and programs like it are not an option for most families, but it does give hope and direction for those who want to find healing and a better future for their children without having to resort to drugs in schools that want to force a square peg into a round hole. The newest percentages of children being labeled with so-called ADHD or ADD, reported in January 2022, show that the numbers are increasing dramatically, and at younger and younger ages.[152]

- 6.1 million children ages 2-17 are labeled with the lie ADHD. That is nearly 10% of the population of children in the United States!
- Of that number, adolescents, ages 12-17, number 3.3 million being labeled, which is 13.6 % of that population.
- Of that number, boys make up 12.9 %, while girls only make up 5.6 %.
- 62 percent of children ages 2-17 labeled with ADHD are currently taking so called ADHD medication. Of that number:
- 18.2 percent of 2 to 5 year-olds are labeled with ADHD.

- 68.6 percent of 6-11 year olds are labeled with ADHD.
- 62.1 percent of 12-17 year olds are labeled with ADHD
- Nearly two-thirds of children labeled with ADHD have at least one other condition such as behavioral problems, anxiety, depression, learning disabilities, tourette syndrome, etc.
- Adults labeled with ADHD are growing four times faster than children labeled with ADHD in the United States, having a **26.4% increase** among children compared to **123.3% increase** among adults.

These numbers are frightening. Everyone should be aghast that 18% of children in the United States **from age 2-5** are being labeled with ADHD and being given drugs, that is really dope, to calm them down. And why suddenly are adults being labeled with ADHD? **123% increase???** Our Lady said:

March 2, 2009

> **"... I am here among you. I am looking into your wounded and restless hearts. You have become lost, my children..."**

Zack was described as "restless" before he was helped in finding a way to transform his restlessness into productive living. Williams laments the situation stating:

> *"We have come to see* ***the restlessness that was once adaptive as a pathology.*** *A recent advertisement for an ADHD drug listed the 'symptoms' to watch for:* ***'May climb or run excessively, have trouble staying seated.'"*** [153]

If all this makes you angry, it should. Righteous anger is a legitimate reaction to the legalization of a serious crime.

The simple answer of how we got ourselves in this mess in the first place is that children have lost their connection to the natural world. The last chapter laid out what nature gives to man. As you have already read, God sourced into wind, light, rushing water, birdsong, twinkling stars, the aroma of honeysuckle and pine, blue skies and purple mountains, and a trillion other elements in nature healing for man, his soul and his spirit. If this is true for man, it is doubly so for children. But children's loss of nature comes with it a danger that adults do not necessarily have. Most adults still have the memory of nature, even if they live a life that is mostly indoors, and therefore can still connect to the world God created. But children who do not have early exposure to nature, are likely never to grow to seek it out, but will rather fear the unknown that nature will become for them.

Why does that matter? It matters because a child will not reach his full potential without direct exposure to nature. It is essential for a child's physical and emotional development. There is a growing amount of research linking the lack of nature in the lives of children and the rise in depression, obesity, anxiety, behavioral problems, etc. Children have a natural impulse for exploring and adventure. When that is not allowed expression in a child's life, a part of that child shrivels up and dies. Surviving becomes the goal in life, not thriving.

In Richard Louv's ground-breaking book, Last Child in the Woods, he states:

> *"In an agricultural society, or during a time of exploration and settlement, or hunting and fathering—which is to say, most of mankind's history—energetic boys were particularly prized for their strength, speed and agility... As recently as the 1950s, most families still had some kind of agricultural connection. Many of these children, girls as well as boys, would have been directing their energy and physicality in constructive ways: doing farm chores, baling hay, splashing in the swimming hole,*

> *climbing trees, racing to the sandlot for a game of baseball. Their unregimented play would have been steeped in nature."* [154]

But that world has all but passed away. What do we have as a replacement? A world in which children become more and more confined to smaller and smaller spaces. This begins in "babyhood," with babies spending more and more time "strapped in" to car seats and other restraints. (A terrible thing, but the way of life has made this a necessity.) University of Maryland professor, Jane Clark, coined the phrase, "containerized kids."

> *"Most kid-containerizing is done for safety concerns, but the long-term health of these children is compromised."* [155]

What is compromised?

> *"...risks to physical and psychological health, risk to children's concept and perception of*

> *community, risk to self-confidence and the ability to discern true danger."* [156]

And then again, the natural curiosity of the world around them is often stunted because of the inability to be able to explore. What a travesty that is because exploration is how God made children to learn. Frustration builds within a child who cannot express this natural impulse and the child therefore reacts with tantrums, misbehavior, focus and attention problems. These are the very behaviors that will lead to, even at a very young age, a Salem witch hunt burning, but not with fire, rather burning up with stimulants and amphetamines, those who are accused, "You are ADHD. We will burn up your life."

This is one of the most atrocious schemes and entire nations should rise up and go after those who propagated and profited from it. Even rats that are restricted from being able to freely explore and play do not grow properly. They develop *"play hunger,"* that leads to *"impulse control problems and eventually problems with social interactions."* [157]

> *"The real disorder is less in the child than it is in the imposed, artificial environment. Viewed from this angle, the society that has disengaged the child from nature is most certainly disordered…To take nature and natural play away from children may be tantamount to withholding oxygen."* [158]

Returning again to Our Lady's March 2, 2009, message, look what She says is the real problem today:

March 2, 2009

> **"…I am here among you. I am looking into your wounded and restless hearts. You have become lost, my children. Your wounds from sin are becoming greater and greater and are <u>distancing you all the more from the real truth</u>…"**

What is the "real truth" Our Lady is speaking of here? It is the fact that man has created an artificial environment around our children in which so many of them are not able to succeed or thrive.

Florence Williams ponders in The Nature Fix:

> *"I had to wonder if we are cutting them off at the knees, not just with medication, but through overstructured, overmanaged classrooms and sports teams, less freedom to roam and ever-more-dazzling indoor seductions."* [159]

And ever-more-dazzling and demonic seductions are coming our way.

There is no sign that the world is going to be reversing its course anytime soon. That will take an act of God through the Secrets promised through Our Lady of Medjugorje. Divine intervention "IS COMING," but until then, we have responsibilities to change this diabolical direction. For those who wake to the horror of what is going on, how our children have been used as guinea pigs, it's time to get out of the burning building before it collapses upon you. Get out of cities, build an agrarian way of life, homeschool or start a neighborhood school. Take control of your lives again—and get your kids into God's Creation where they will find healing, strength, creativity, peace and sanity again. Williams' research led her to this very important conclusion:

> *"The future will belong to the nature-smart-those individuals, families, businesses and political leaders who develop a deeper understanding of the transformative power of the natural world and who balance the virtual with the real. The more high-tech we become, the more nature we need."*[160]

"FYI—The use of antidepressant drugs in the USA between 1991 and 2018 has increased by a dramatic ***3,000%!*** *Antidepressant prescriptions have increased by over 20% since COVID-19 started in 2020. We cannot ignore the correlation between the increase in violent crime and mass shootings with the number of mentally ill individuals who are clearly recognized by so many around them who are aware of their intention to harm. No gun control laws will ever fix this problem."*

Country Western Singer,
Travis Tritt on Twitter

CONCLUSION—PART I

Do Not Remain Paralyzed

Make War

Everyone knows that those who are killed or wounded from school or other mass shootings are victims. But as already stated, and as this book has proven, most shooters are also victims. There is an "overdose" of evidence in this book that suicidal and murderous thoughts overpower individuals' rationality and reality, due to the drugs that have been prescribed to them. Out of the millions who are fed their daily ration of Ritalin, Prozac, Adderall, and other psychotropic drugs, who will be the next to lose their rational thinking? All conned by pharmaceutical companies for the phantom made-up defects known as ADD, ADHD, etc., so-called disorders that are "treated" with dangerous and debilitating drugs.

If you are in need of more proof of what has been revealed here, just as this book was going to print a bombshell study came out in July 2022, confirming yet again that *"the 'chemical imbalance' theory — that depression is due to a lack of the brain chemical serotonin — is nothing more than a myth."*[156] The report goes on to say:

> *"In the most comprehensive review of the research on links between depression and serotonin ever carried out, researchers from the UK, Italy and Switzerland looked at 17 major international reviews that had documented the findings from more than 260 studies, involving 300,000 patients. Their findings, published in the journal Molecular Psychiatry, undermine the basis for decades of prescribing of the most commonly used antidepressants, Selective Serotonin Reuptake Inhibitors, or SSRIs."*[157]

Professor Joanna Moncrieff, the head of the research group and a respected consultant psychiatrist, gave her name to the findings in which it was stated that they *"found 'no convincing evidence' of a link between the mental illness and serotonin levels."*[158] Moncrieff, her team and their research were immediately attacked by top doctors as being "absurd" and "grossly exaggerated." Moncrieff responded to these criticisms bluntly, saying:

> *"People are told the reason they feel depressed is that there is something wrong with the chemistry in their brain and antidepressants could put it right. But if there's no evidence there's anything wrong with the brain's chemistry, then that doesn't sound like a sensible solution. This profession has misled people for so long about the need for antidepressants and now doctors don't want to admit they got it wrong."*[159]

Findings released in yet another study was just as revealing in that researchers looked at 17.5 million US adults with depression over a 10 year period, in which half were taking medication and half were not. Results showed a slight improvement in mental health *in both groups*, regardless of whether they were on antidepressants. The fact that there was no statistical difference between those taking the medication and those who weren't, the study suggests that using antidepressants does not significantly improve the quality of life over time. Some believe the antidepressants work as a placebo effect, they feel better because they believe the drug is correcting a chemical imbalance — which, as this book has exposed, is not true; there is no imbalance.[160]

This leads us back to where we began. Millions are taking SSRIs [**S**elective **S**erotonin **R**euptake **I**nhibitors] to fix something in themselves that is not broken. Yet, they become broken through the side effects of these psychotropic drugs, especially if they are experiencing brokenness in their families. It becomes an equation that leads to catastrophes.

Psychotropic Drugs

Family problems

+ satan

Equals: Catastrophes

Mind-altering psychotropic drugs inflame family problems. satan provides the gasoline with these two ingredients to wear down and weaken wounded hearts to the point where catastrophes happen. Is there a study supporting this paragraph? Do you need one? The wisdom of common sense proves the truth of what is stated in the above equation. So, let's take a look at some of these individuals who fell in the category of having extreme side effects when under the influence of SSRIs. Remember as you read their stories, the current research resulting in the review of millions of individuals who have taken psychotropic drugs for decades is exposing the lie behind these drugs.

Ethan Crumbley, a 15-year-old from Michigan, shot and killed four students in his school on November 30, 2021. He complained about seeing demons and hearing voices. The day of the shooting, his school counselor was alerted that Ethan was watching a shooting video and a short time later school officials were told that Ethan had drawn disturbing pictures on a math test, described by the New York Times:

> *"The note contained the following: a drawing of a semiautomatic handgun, pointing at the words: 'The thoughts won't stop. Help me.' In another section of the note was a drawing of a bullet, with the following words above that bullet: 'Blood everywhere.' Between the drawing of the gun and the bullet is a drawing of a person who appears to have been shot twice and bleeding. Below that figure is a drawing of a laughing emoji. Further down the drawing are the words, 'My life is useless.' And to*

the right of that are the words, 'The world is dead.'"[166] [167]

Ethan's parents were called to the school. When they arrived, the counselor said, *"They didn't seem friendly or show care, and they didn't seem to comfort their son with a hug."*[168]

The school wanted, but did not insist, that the Crumbley's take Ethan out of school and take him home. Instead, the parents left him in school which turned out to be a fatal mistake as Ethan had the gun used in the shooting spree hidden in his locker. The parents were arrested for manslaughter when the judge presiding over the case declared that the shooting could have been avoided and was, in part, due to parental neglect. In his journal, Ethan wrote that he was tired of, "fighting with my dark side," which was leading him to "shoot up" the school.[169] He wrote in bold letters, crying out, **"Help me."**

Ethan Crumbley was not the only shooter who "heard voices" compelling him to kill. It is common among many of the shooters. What is also common is that the majority of shooters have a history of being medicated on antidepressants and other dangerous drugs. Specifically, they are the kind of drugs that induce suicidal and homicidal thoughts and impulses; hence the "hearing of voices." What does this mean exactly? How do simple thoughts, even voices, lead to triggering someone to commit, the most heinous of crimes? In his article, *"Was Ethan Crumbley on Prozac?,"* author Fred Gardner delves more deeply into the mindset of those who have experienced these strong temptations towards suicide and homicide. He writes:

> *"'Suicidal ideation,' 'Suicide gesture,' 'Suicide attempt,' and other such terms do not accurately characterize the extremely bizarre*

> *flip-outs induced by SSRIs** [**S**elective **S**erotonin **R**euptake **I**nhibitors]. *Carefully planning to annihilate the student body fits the profile.* [Thoughts of] *Biting your mother 57 times.* [Thoughts of] *Driving your car around in circles until you smash into a tree* [fits the profile]…*"*[170]

These are just a few real examples of the haunting thoughts that imprison individuals under the influence of SSRIs, the most commonly prescribed antidepressants. Gardner also relays in his article the testimony of Bonnie Leitsch, founder of The Prozac Survivors Support Group, who testified before the FDA Psychopharmacologic Drugs Advisory Hearings on September 20, 1991. The FDA hearings were convened because of the increasing number of reports pointing to a causation between suicides and homicides and psychotropic drugs that

* **S**elective **S**erotonin **R**euptake **I**nhibitors are a class of drugs that are typically used as antidepressants in the treatment of major depression, anxiety and other psychological conditions.

the FDA had approved. Leitsch spoke from experience, having taken Prozac herself. She gives a vivid description of the confusing private world created in her mind when under the influence of Prozac:

> *"It's hard for people to understand. They say, 'you must know what you're doing,' but you do not. You cannot distinguish reality. I could never tell if I was awake or asleep. That was the hardest thing for me to determine. I would lay down in bed and I would think 'Now am I dreaming this or am I awake and doing this?' My mind constantly ran, it never would stop. I could be having this conversation with you and the whole time if I was drinking coffee, I could be thinking about running it on my hand* [the coffee] *and wondering what it would feel like. Thinking irrational thoughts. And yet still able to communicate at what would appear to be a rational level. That's why I think psychiatrists and psychologists*

and doctors who are dealing with people on Prozac are totally oblivious to what's going on. These people [those taking the drugs] *are the best liars in the whole world in terms of being able to come to you and say, 'I'm fine.' But the whole time they might be thinking 'I wonder what it would feel like to stick this knife in my hand?' And, 'I can take on a motorcycle gang and kill 'em all.' Most of these people on Prozac like myself* ***lose all natural ability to love. It becomes a spiritual dullness. You cease to know right from wrong.*** *Because there's no wrong and you're right 100 percent and the h--- with the rest of you."*[171]

During her testimony at the FDA Psychopharmacologic Drugs Advisory Hearings, Leitsch explained how thoughts of suicide, while under the influence of the drug, come suddenly, without provocation, warning or even visual or other detectable psychotic behavior, making it impossible to "monitor" a patient on the drug.

> *"Doctors say that this problem with Prozac, all that is needed is for this drug to be monitored. But what I'd like to know is how do you monitor a patient when suddenly and without warning they try to take their lives? Such as the woman in North Carolina who was cooking supper, had a load of clothes in the washer and dryer, no indication that she was going to commit suicide but, indeed, she did. She hanged herself with a belt in the middle of cooking supper. Now how can you monitor that? Likewise, the man in Arizona, laid out his medication for the day, played gin rummy with his wife, made plans for the day, and while she was taking a shower he killed himself. How do you monitor that? And myself, my own case.* ***I was making icing for a Father's Day cake when suddenly, without***

> ***warning, it seemed like a swell idea to kill myself.*** *Did I consider the consequences of that? No. Did I shoot myself? No, because a gun wasn't handy. Had it been handy, I'm sure I would have done that.* [Instead, she swallowed a bottle of pain killers.] *I was, however, dead on arrival to the hospital. Had it not been for the emergency team* [who saved her life], *I would not be here."*[172]

In the summer of 1989, Bonnie Leitsch swallowed one bottle of pain pills and then a second bottle when it was taking too long to end her life. She was pronounced dead upon arrival at the hospital, but was able to be revived by the emergency room medical team. This was the incident that moved her to make public her traumatic experience, whereupon she began to be contacted by hundreds of others around the nation with similar horrific experiences with Prozac and other mind-altering prescription drugs.

Reading Leitsch's testimony, one cannot take lightly the testimonies of those who committed the grievous murders that have rocked our nation over the past 20 years in which the killers were under the influence of similar drugs. As this book is being finished, Parkland, Florida shooter, Nikolas Cruz, is sitting in a court room where the decision will be made whether or not he will be sentenced to death for the 17 people he killed and the dozens that he injured on February 14, 2018. Most people will have no mercy for Cruz and will demand his death. But Cruz was a patient at Broward County's largest mental health service provider, Henderson Behavioral Health. It is very likely that he was taking psychotropic drugs. He told investigators just after the shooting spree that he heard voices in his head, giving him instructions on what to do to conduct the attack. He described the voices as "demons."[173]

What if it was the drug that induced Cruz to kill? Another question that begs to be asked: Why is the public allowed to know even the smallest details of everything that led up to Cruz's actions on February 14, 2018, but is not allowed to know if he was on psychotropic drugs due to "medical privacy" laws, which do not allow the light to shine in the shadows. By now you, the reader, can conclude that something very dirty, very evil has transpired when one sees the passing of a law for medical privacy coincides to the time period when the evidence starts to accumulate, pointing to a connection between the increasing numbers of suicides and homicides to the increasing numbers of those on psychotropic medication.

On November 3, 1999, a proposed rule for "medical privacy," including those with mental illness or those under the care of a psychiatrist, was placed before Congress. The law was ratified by Congress on December 28, 2000. Coincidentally, the proposal came just six months after the Columbine High School shooting, in which it was widely reported that the shooter, Eric Harris, was on the antidepressant drug, Luvox. His accomplice, Dylan Klebold, was reportedly on Paxil and Zoloft, though Klebold's medical records have remained sealed, like so many others who have committed similar crimes in recent years. Use your common sense. Who would want to cover up medical records? Why?

The September 20, 1991, FDA hearing resulted in the continued protection of the pharmaceutical companies and their multi-billion-dollar industry, foundationed on drugging our young people and destroying their lives. And who gets a piece of that billion-dollar pie as long as they stay silent and do not allow the public to get wind of what is really going on? Congressmen? Doctors? Scientists? Universities? Lawyers? Judges? Only a one-word sentence describes those complicit in this crime. Diabolical.

And what about the fake-news conglomerates? After Ethan Crumbley's shooting spree, the news focus was immediately diverted off of Ethan and onto his parents as Fred Gardner noted in his essay, "Was Ethan Crumbley on Prozac?" Gardner stated:

> *"Already the coverage from Michigan is focusing on his parents' politics, not the kid's mental state. The grown-up Crumbleys were obdurate* when the school told them Ethan needed counseling—but it's possible the family doctor had prescribed an SSRI* [**S**elective **S**erotonin **R**euptake **I**nhibitor], *for their unhappy 15-year-old. More than **one** in **20** teenage boys in the U.S. are on antidepressants—and more than **one** in **10** teenage girls."*[174]

Meanwhile, broken individuals, who could never imagine having the capacity to cause so much horror, harm and pain, end their own lives or sit rot-

* Obdurate means stubbornly refusing to change one's opinion or course of action.

ting in prison cells. Here are just a few of the many shooters who described "hearing voices," who lost the ability to love, have empathy or compassion when medicated to death while their body is still alive. The shooters say they could not silence the voices, that led to the tragic taking of lives, and in some cases taking their own lives.

Conner Betts: August 4, 2019. Dayton, Ohio. Betts was prescribed the single most prescribed psychiatric medication used to treat anxiety and panic disorder: Xanax. Nine people were killed, including his brother, and 17 people were wounded. Anxiety is very often related to family problems. Betts "had heard menacing voices in his head since he was young, and talked about "dark, evil things," his ex-girlfriend said. He was a serious and reserved kid who struggled with hallucinations. Betts said he'd long suffered from psychosis and feared developing schizophrenia.[175]

Aaron Alexis: September 16, 2013. Washington, D.C. Alexis was taking the antidepressant drug, Trazodone. Twelve people were killed, three people were injured. Rhode Island Police warned the U.S. Navy that the Washington Navy Yard gunman, Aaron Alexis, had reported "hearing voices." Alexis told police he believed people were following him and "sending vibrations into his body."[176]

Waid Anthony Melton: November 12, 2018. Warehouse in Albuquerque, New Mexico. When Melton, who had a history of mental illness, called 911 after the shooting, he confessed that he was the active shooter who seriously injured three of his coworkers. He said he had been hearing voices since he was 15. A call to 911 is a call, a cry, for help. He was going to silence the voices. He killed himself with a gunshot wound.[177]

No name: February 14, 2019. Albuquerque, New Mexico. Police say a 16-year-old boy accused of firing a gun at a New Mexico high school told officers

11 months prior voices were telling him to "shoot up the school."[178]

Estebon Santiago: January 6, 2017. Fort Lauderdale International Airport in Broward County, Florida. Five people were killed, six people were injured in shooting. Santiago was an Iraq War Veteran with a history of mental illness. Santiago was being treated in Alaska after complaining of hearing voices and had recently claimed his mind was being controlled by a U.S. intelligence Agency and that the CIA was forcing him to watch ISIS videos. In prison, he refused to take the psychotropic medicine prescribed to him.[179] Perhaps Santiago feared the effects that he knew the drug would have on him.

Darion Marcus Aguilar: January 24, 2014. Mall in Marriotsville, Maryland. Two people were killed. Aguilar was obsessed with the Columbine High School shooting. Police said that he heard voices and struggled with mental illness. The morning of the shooting he woke up and "felt no emotions, no empathy, no sympathy." Again, just as Leitsch said in her testimony, "*Most of these people on Prozac like myself* ***lose all natural ability to love.***"[180]

Kip Kinkel: May 21, 1998. School in Springfield, Oregon. Killed four people (including his parents), injured 25 people. Kinkel testified that there were voices screaming in his head which drove him to shoot his father in the back of the head and kill his mother just after he told her he loved her. The voices pushed him to load a rifle and two pistols, head for Thurston High School and open fire on the crowded cafeteria. The voices got louder and harder to resist as Kinkel became more depressed and stressed. The voices peaked when he was expelled from school for having a gun in his locker—the same day he shot his father and his mother. "But I have to kill people," he wrote before taking his guns to school. "I don't know why. I am so sorry."[181]

James Holmes: July 20, 2012. Aurora, Colorado. Killed 12 people, wounded 70 people. Holmes thought obsessively about killing people in the months before he opened fire in a crowded movie theater. The psychiatrist Holmes was seeing, Dr. Lynne Fenton, testified that Holmes told her in March 2012 that he had **"homicidal thoughts"** – as often as three or four times a day. As his treatment progressed, he told her his obsession with killing was only getting worse. The diagnosis evolved over several sessions, and she later saw signs of paranoia and psychosis. She spoke with his mother and came to believe his homicidal thoughts were longstanding, dating back to childhood. After their fourth session on April 17, she noted that he made several odd statements she didn't understand and wrote in her notes, "psychotic level thinking?"[182]

Aaron Ybarra: June 5, 2014. Shooting occurred at Seattle Pacific University. One person killed, two people injured. He had a history of mental illness, was seeing a psychotherapist and was prescribed medications. Ybarra testified that God and satan had a secret plan to get him to commit a mass shooting on a university campus. He talked about hearing the voice of Eric Harris, one of two students responsible for the 1999 shootings at Columbine High School in Colorado.[183]

Where were such atrocious things decades ago? One ingredient to these mass killings that was not available back then are the many psychotropic drugs such as Ritalin, Adderall, Prozac, etc., available today. Parkland shooter, Nikolas Cruz, at his trial, pled guilty and said, *"I have to live with this every day, and it brings me nightmares and I can't live with myself sometimes,"*[184] in an apology he made to the families of the victims he had killed to express his regret at what he had done. He said he was following the voices that told him to ***"Burn. Kill. Destroy."***[185] Even Stephen Paddock, the Las Vegas shooter, an adult, who killed 60 people and injured 413 people in one of the most horrific mass shootings in the history of the U.S., was found to have psychiatric drugs in his system at the time of the shooting. One close to him said that there were times he would be lying in bed screaming to himself. Investigators believe the shooter may have been in "physical or mental anguish."[186]

Many shooters, as well as those who have committed similar crimes with other weapons, have testified that they did not want to carry out the heinous actions they committed, but they could not get the thoughts out of their heads to kill. Again, where were these, no motive, ruthless, useless shootings decades ago? Why suddenly do we hear of shootings everywhere? As you have read, and to purposely be repetitive to help you go deeper into your thoughts, you do not have to have a university sponsored study to draw a valid conclusion. Common sense and reason lead one to the conclusion that something has triggered the explosion of shootings, suicides and homicides, especially among the youth in our time. These incidences coincide with the increased propagation and promotion of the "urgent mandate" to parents that they must save their children through putting them on the psychotropic drugs, Ritalin, Adderall, or any of the other profitable "devil's brew." How else could you explain how the increase of suicides and homicides (ie. mass shootings, etc.) is parallelling the increase of the marketing of these prescription psychotropic drugs?

DECLARE WAR against those predators who do not bend their knee to God, rather they bend to the god of money.

In September 1991, Bonnie Leitsch, in her testimony before the FDA Psychopharmacologic Drugs Advisory Hearings, did not hold back in her fury of what the FDA and pharmaceutical companies had unleashed upon the public. In her testimony, Leitsch, who herself is a survivor of a suicide attempt induced by the drug, Prozac, said:

"What I'm curious about is the people who seem to think it's perfectly okay to have this drug on the market are people who have a vested interest. I question why this is happening. Well, we know it's impossible for the doctors to monitor these patients, because if they had, there would not have been 800 suicides, 500 deaths associated with this drug. And if all of this isn't tragic enough, we are referred to as* ***anecdotal*** (meaning according to or by means of personal accounts rather than facts or research). *What does that mean? Does that mean that the people that died on this drug are not equally as dead? Does it mean that Sally Padoor, who's grieving the loss of her son, is not just as grieved? I think not. What that really means is that we were not in the paid-for studies of Eli Lilly (pharmaceutical company). We are the real people. Anecdotes are the real people. We are the people that*

* Since September 1991 when this hearing was held.

you have unleashed this drug on. The FDA responsibility – now, maybe we need to make this a little more clear – is to protect the general public, not to stuff money into doctors' and into Eli Lilly's pocket at the expense of the general public. How dare you? You were put here to protect us. We are the general public. And who said it's okay, who in the world said it is okay to kill one person so that another feels better? Who gives anyone here that right? ***Where in this country is it all right for you to say it only kills 3.5 percent?*** *Gentlemen, if you want to be that 3.5 percent, fine, have at it. But the general public does not want to be that 3.5 percent."*[187]

Bonnie Leitsch called those she spoke to on the FDA Advisory Board, "gentlemen," as a courtesy, when in fact, **many of the members on the advisory committee were receiving funding from antidepressant manufacturers.**[188] What then was the result of the hearing in considering whether SSRIs [**S**elective **S**erotonin **R**euptake **I**nhibitor], can induce violent and suicidal thoughts?

> ***"They voted 9–0 <u>not</u> <u>to</u> <u>recommend</u> a more prominent warning and 6–3 <u>not</u> <u>to</u> <u>recommend</u> a warning in small type*** *that would have read, 'In a small number of patients, depressive symptoms have worsened during therapy, including the emergence of suicidal thoughts and attempts. Surveillance throughout treatment is recommended.'"*[189]

This FDA Advisory Board, along with the pharmaceutical CEOs, board members, the doctors who prescribe these medicines, etc., may look nice in their suits, in high-up positions of their companies and labs and government offices, etc., but beware; they are worse than wolves in sheep's clothing. Worse? What does that mean? Christ tells us how bad this is when, for decades, they have produced a product that wrongfully causes the death of self, death of others, and damage for life to the little ones, those children who were led astray. These drugs are altering the natural behavior of millions of children between the ages of 3 to 17, which does not include the millions of adults who also are underneath the influence of these satanic drugs. Christ says:

> ***"It would be better for you if a millstone were hung around your neck and you were thrown into the sea than for you to cause one of these little ones to stumble."*** Luke 17:12

More and more evidence has been found over the past two decades to show a definite causation between psychotropic drugs and an increase in suicidal and homicidal ideation in young people, yet the drug companies continue to do everything to hide this truth from the public. It is unconscionable and criminal.

Begin now. You must go on the attack with this book. It is your weapon. Spread it at your work, your church, on social media, to your sheriffs, school boards, school principals, parent groups, city counsels, every avenue that you can. Call all local and nationwide talk shows on radio. Meet with others and discuss what actions you can take. **Do not look to the government for help.** The Food and Drug Administration (FDA) is complicit (along with other government agencies) and is known for *"the revolving door,"* meaning individuals from the FDA are offered high salary positions in the companies that the FDA regulate over. On the other side, the regulated companies have their employees hired at the FDA. Often these employees and government officials are from the same family (ie. spouses, siblings, etc.).

While the FDA is supposed to be protecting the public from food and drugs that are harmful, in reality they are often involved in back-street deals and payoffs that grease the wheels for approval and protect the interests of the private companies, rather than the public. The same kind of relationship also exists between the pharmaceutical companies and the mainstream media. How else do you explain the silence and lack of curiosity of the reporters to even ask the question if the shooters are on psychotropic drugs. As investigative reporter, David Kupelin, said earlier, pharmaceutical companies do not want any "free publicity of this sort."[190] It is why they are by far the biggest sponsors of television news. Media pressure could force the opening of medical records to be able to examine whether a correlation exists between these drugs and the shooters.

But, while the mainstream media bypasses this crucial story, there have been many "citizen journalists," who are asking the hard questions and are finding a strong correlation between big pharma drugs and the shooters in mass shootings.

These relationships give private companies great influence over the FDA, EPA, Department of Agriculture, mainstream media, etc. That is why, do not look for government to help. Bypass the government and take the war into your own hands. You, as an individual, can act. You can also take action with others, forming groups. How?

Three Steps of Actions

1. **Starting the War.** Not everyone can financially afford to take this step but there are a lot of wealthy people whose children are on these mind-altering chemicals/drugs who can sue the pharmaceutical companies, their CEOs, Boards of Directors, including employees that know the tragic damage that these drugs are doing from preschool children all the way up to adults. When evidence first started to manifest that Prozac (and other copycat drugs) were having adverse reactions among those who were taking

the drug, the manufacturer, Eli Lilly's *"strategy was to conceal the trend by settling every case out of court."*[191] The cover up continues today, even though they eventually were forced to put on the prescription labels a statement that these drugs can and have incited suicidal and murderous thoughts.

But, how does a little statement in tiny print grant immunity? That minimal caution does not excuse murder and many other damaging side effects. If you put poison in a glass of water knowing whoever drinks it will die, or at the very least, their health will be damaged for life, you cannot plead "I didn't know" the harm it would cause when evidence proves you had knowledge of what you were doing? Clearly it is murder. It is simply an arithmetic problem as 1 + 1 = 2. This is not complicated. Recommending and selling a drug that suggests killing oneself and others is a causation for investigations that will result in arrest warrants. Executives of mega-pharmaceutical companies have built a wall of immunity around themselves. Now that this evil is being exposed, no one should just stand still with their hands in their pockets. Channel your righteous anger, your resources, your concern for all into action. These shootings and other tragic events can be stopped by you.

YOUR MANUAL FOR ACTION IS THE BOOK YOU ARE HOLDING IN YOUR HAND

Put your actions into God's hands. The Virgin Mary said:

May 25, 2019

> **"...pray to be worthy instruments in God's hands..."**

December 25, 2017

> **"...surrender your lives into God's hands..."**

The more you spread this book, the more people will join together and form an army united by a common cause by and through the natural instinct of being protectors of the "little ones."

YOUR COUNTY SHERIFF HAS AUTHORITY TO STOP DEAD THIS GENOCIDE OF THE MIND

2. **Demand Warrants.** The book, The David Answer*, lays out how county sheriffs have absolute protection and constitutional authority over all citizens in their counties. They are the supreme law enforcement official that supersedes state and federal agents' authority. This authority creates a duty in the office of the sheriff to be a defender of the rights of the people and not a blind enforcer of the law. Most sheriffs either do not know about this power and duty or they refuse to exercise the full power granted to them in their office.

* The David Answer was written by a Friend of Medjugorje in 2012. See the order form in the back of the book. Or call Caritas of Birmingham at 205-672-2000, or order on their website, Mej.com.

Sheriffs have the independent authority and the duty to investigate pharmaceutical companies, their CEOs, Board of Directors, etc., for any alleged aiding and abetting murder, suicide and the mental anguish that causes life-long damage, when wounded by or experiencing the trauma from witnessing a shooting takes place. Parents and concerned citizens should meet with their local sheriffs and demand sheriffs investigate, file criminal complaints, and request warrants against those who have unlawfully damaged and/or destroyed their children's lives. County sheriffs need to educate themselves and then investigate how psychotropic drugs are the root cause of almost all of these mass homicides. It is worth repeating, many sheriffs, as well as civilians, do not understand the power, authority, and duty the sheriff has to stop the abuse of power by every agency in the federal and state governments.

Alongside the book, Has satan Pulled Another One on You?, the book, The David Answer, is critical to read and spread to educate yourselves and others that the elected protectors, "by the people," places county sheriffs in the supreme position to uphold your constitutional rights, above the federal and state officials, and even above the courts. Groups should meet with their sheriffs and hold them accountable. Tell your sheriff that these two books can stop many shootings. Give your sheriff and the police chief of your city both books. Drill into yourself, and all who you know, that sheriffs are elected by the people to support and defend your constitutional rights and all those of all the citizens in your county.

Homeschoolers should be taught these truths, but also, a good constitutional sheriff can see that these truths are also taught in public and private schools. If your sheriff does not act strongly, tell him you will begin working to elect a new sheriff. Another option is to run for the position of sheriff of your county yourself. You do not have to have any training; you only need to know the U.S. Constitution. This cannot be overstated. The power, authority, and duty of a county sheriff is enormous and is one of the keys for stopping the shootings and the drugs that are destroying millions of lives of the youth and adults in this nation.

CREATE A TSUNAMI

3. **File massive numbers of lawsuits.** The lawsuits are not only about winning individual cases. The purpose is to shut down these mega pharmaceutical companies producing these drugs. They are extremely powerful, but there are millions of people with children whose litigation can break these companies financially for what they have done, as well as having criminal charges lev-

eled at the top tier of these companies as mentioned—CEOs, Board Members, etc. Your number one priority is to spread this book. This book has the information to force these people out of business and into serious prison time. It is about literally breaking the pharmaceutical companies by having millions of lawsuits to fight, so many lawsuits filed as to sink them like a brick tied around their necks and thrown to the bottom of the sea. It is not time to be nice. It is time for war. What these people, who are in the know, propagated and promoted for money is diabolical, and they need to go to prison.

Diabolical – Prison?

According to the Centers for Disease Control and Prevention (CDC):[192]

A. The number of 10–14 year olds who took their own lives nearly tripled from 2007 to 2017.

B. In the U.S., suicide is the second leading cause of death among children and adolescents ages 10–24.

C. Suicide is the third leading cause of death among 12 year olds.

D. In at least one state, Ohio, suicide has become the number one leading cause of death for children ages 10–14.

It is unfathomable that so many children so young could want to end their lives. Or did they want to? What led these little ones astray?

Is There Enough To Mount An Army?

Answer: Yes!

Where will the people come from?

A. There are an estimated **18.5 million 3- to 5-year old children** in the U.S. Out of that number, **1.2 %** are on psychiatric medication. That amounts to there being **222,000** 3–5 year olds, practically babies, being destroyed of their lives who may end up also destroying others.[193]

B. There are an estimated **24.3 million 6–11 year-old children** in the U.S. Out of that number, **7.6 %** are on psychiatric medication. That amounts to there being **1,846,800** 6–11 year olds, little children being destroyed of their lives who may end up also destroying others.[194]

C. There are an estimated **25.1 million 12–17 year old children** in the U.S. Out of that number, **12.9%** are on psychiatric medicines. That amounts to there being **3,237,900** 12–17 year olds, children in their youth, being destroyed of their lives who may end up also destroying others.[195]

The total number of youth in the U.S. endangered: **Five million, one hundred sixty-nine thousand, twenty-nine children, from ages 3–17 who are taking psychiatric medications.**

Can you attack this genocide of the mind? Consider the following: About 7% of the U.S. population earns more than $1 million a year; $1.9 million is the threshold that defines who is "wealthy." The average American family has two children under the age of 18. While there are many children who have been harmed by these drugs, whose families cannot afford to file a lawsuit, there are attorneys that can file personal injury lawsuits with no cost as attorneys are paid by a percentage when they win the case.

* * * * *

With more than 5, 169,029 kids currently on these drugs who have suffered damages, not to mention the tens of thousands of others who have lost loved ones or who have been injured due to the violence done to them by those on these drugs, the numbers are there to launch a widespread class-action suit. Where will the money come from to file all those lawsuits? Two main sources.

Over the last five years, almost everyone has witnessed the rapid rise in advertising for personal injury lawyers. The billboards are literally everywhere, sometimes stacked one on top of the other. Radio, newspaper, and magazine ads have all gotten in on the action as well. In 2022, the personal injury market is expected to hit about $42.3 billion.[196] It is estimated that currently there are somewhere between 300,000 and 500,000 personal injury lawsuits filed each year.[197]

As a general rule, personal injury law firms collect a percentage based fee at the **end of the case**, and only if they win. A common compensation for personal injury lawyers is equal to 33% of any final settlement the client receives. This gives the attorney a strong financial incentive to fight hard for your case, because if he doesn't win, he doesn't get paid. The more lawsuits that are filed, the more publicity will be given to the cases, and the more attorneys will be eager to take on new lawsuits. It is in their basic financial interest to file these lawsuits.

Doing a lot of reading and looking at history over the centuries, I wrote in They Fired the First Shot 2012, *"It is known that a revolution is caused by 5% of the people. The rest of the 95% will follow."* It is important that people just begin to file these lawsuits to begin building the tsunami and then the economics of the cases and the dynamics of the personal injury market will simply take over. Because personal injury lawyers work on contingent fees (they get paid only if they win), it may be basically free to file **massive** numbers of lawsuits.

The entire personal injury lawsuit infrastructure is already in place. **But the motive to file should not be just for money.** Attorneys first motive should be for the righteous cause of protecting their own and everyone else's children and grandchildren. As these mass shootings demonstrate, everyone is impacted, the whole culture. Attorneys, in their profession, can promote a righteous cause and stop the damage to millions of youth and stop the shootings!! It is not guns that need to be banned. It is the drugs that need to be banned. The Second Amendment should not be banished. The dangerous psychotic drugs should be banished.

This book, Has satan Pulled Another One on You?, not only exposes this evil, it is a premade legal plan for lawsuit war. The research has been done, and the evidence is already laid out for attorneys. Looking at it from the perspective of someone in this personal injury war, one will quickly grasp the enormous cannon balls that can be fired at these perpetrators and their companies through lawsuits to put youth back on track for their lives. Five million plus children, not counting adults. The damages won for each case, while a victory, will not erase the lifelong damage caused by the drugs. This is why these lawsuit settlements will easily go into the billions of dollars.

"Because drugs have become so profitable, major medical journals rarely publish studies on nondrug treatments of mental health problems. Practitioners who explore treatments are typically marginalized as "alternative." Studies of nondrug treatments are rarely funded unless they involve so-called manualized protocols, where patients and therapists go through narrowly prescribed sequences that allow little fine-tuning to individual patients' needs. Mainstream medicine is firmly committed to a better life through chemistry, and ***the fact that we can actually change our own physiology and inner equilibrium by means other than drugs is rarely considered."***[198]

Bessel van der Kolk,
The Body Keeps the Score: Brain, Mind, and Body in the Healing of Trauma

CONCLUSION—PART II

Are You Going to Stay in Egypt or Start Heading Towards the Promised Land?

Did you know that there were Israelites who did not leave Egypt to follow Moses to the Promised Land? Many of them did not want to turn around from the road they were on. They became accustomed to being with the pagan Egyptians. God wants us today to separate from a pagan culture, just as He called the Israelites to separate from the Egyptians. Common sense, reason and knowing human nature tells us that there were many Israelites who stayed behind, despite the many public miracles that God displayed to build faith in His people to trust Moses, His chosen leader. After 400 years of enslavement under Pharaoh and Egyptian rule, many Israelites had abandoned the faith of Abraham, Isaac and Jacob and instead, assimilated into the way of life of pagan Egypt. The last miracle that God performed that broke the resistance of Pharaoh was when the Angel of Death visited every household whose doorpost wasn't marked by the lamb's blood. The morning broke with great cries of lamentation over the deaths of the first born of every family, including the first born of all their livestock.

When God told the Israelites to mark their doorposts with the lamb's blood, so that the Angel of Death would pass by those households, what if it was for more than just to convince Pharaoh to let His people go. Could God's purpose also have included wanting to find and separate the true Israelites from those who were apostates, those who had abandoned Him for false gods? There were certainly, among the Israelites, those who were unmoved by the drama taking place between Pharaoh and Moses. Those indifferent and cynical Israelites thought Moses was a charlatan. There were those who had given up on God and weren't looking to be saved. The killing of the first born of every family got the attention of not only Pharaoh, but of all the Israelites, both those who had listened to and those who had not listened to God's voice through His servant, Moses. Perhaps there were last minute converts that joined the caravan leaving Egypt because of that sorrowful chastisement brought about by a miracle. But, there were also those who watched millions of their own people pack up and leave—no doubt some from their own families, while they made the decision to stay.

80 Percent!

The Talmud, which means "learning" in Hebrew, is a collection of ancient texts which are important in Judaism. The Talmud states that as much as **80 percent of the Jews never even left Egypt!**[199] How could that be? For some, the Egyptian culture was so ingrained in them that they were unwilling to join the Exodus. Others were afraid of following Moses into the desert. How would they survive? Where would they get food and water? What if they encountered enemies or became ill? How could they defend themselves? While Egypt was not the place they wanted to be, and was even a place they despised, many reasoned it was better than dying in the desert. The mindset can be compared to those who responded or did not respond to Our Lady's call.

Following Our Lady into the desert of Her messages is a dying to self. The call of Moses fell upon many who had no faith, no trust in what their eyes had seen and their ears had heard of how God was using Moses to break the bonds of Israel from Egypt. Regardless of what their reasons were to stay, one thing was certain. They were lost from the Jewish nation forever. Today, with Our Lady, it will be the same. For years, in following Our Lady's messages, we have found answers for today's difficulties that play out as they did in Biblical times. Our Lady said:

May 2, 2014

> **"...And you, my children? Small is the number of those who understand and follow me. Great is the number of those who are lost—of those who have not yet become cognizant of the truth in my Son..."**

Those Israelites who made the decision to stay in Egypt, chose safety and security over being a part of the Greatest Adventure of all time. No doubt, they had listened to "lying voices" and "fake news" that rang out through Egypt, sounding the alarm not to follow Moses, that it was a trick, fake news, that it would lead to certain death. So they stayed...and they missed out on finding the Promised Land. Our Lady said:

February 2, 2018

"...do not believe lying voices..."

I wrote Has satan Pulled Another One on You?, to expose to you, the reader, the "lying voices" of which Our Lady speaks. **Do not use fact-checkers.** They are disinformation platforms for the Left. You must be your own fact-checkers of every voice out there and learn to discern wisely. Isaiah says:

> ***"Come now, let us reason together, says the Lord...If you are willing and obedient, you shall eat the good of the land; but if you refuse and rebel, you shall be eaten by the sword; for the mouth of the Lord has spoken."*** 1:18–20

I have given you so many examples in this book of Our Lady's messages for you to break open truth, through this new language of Our Lady. You must put them into life to have life. If not, you will lose your direction. Is the world going in the right direction? Are you seeing light at the end of the tunnel yet? Why is self-annihilation of one's life the third highest cause of death among those 12–19 years of age, and the second highest cause of death in the same age group is homicide? Does that sound like we are eating the good of the land, or are we rather being killed by the sword?

The purpose of this book is not only to make you feel uncomfortable, **but also angry.** You should feel fed up with agendas being forced on you and your children who are being slaughtered, mentally and physically, by people who do not care for or about your children. As you read in the Conclusion Part I, instructions are given on how to change your ways to defeat these wicked agendas. These monsters only see materialism as a commodity to get rich. It ends with slavery, at the cost of damaging millions upon millions of lives, as well as to enslave not only the youth, but also adults whose "medication" is psychotropic drugs that cause more damaging side affects, worse than the mental problems themselves. Again, as stated in Part I of the Conclusion, we cannot sit on our hands. This heinous crime must be confronted by prison sentences, coupled with civil lawsuits.

I was kneeling shoulder to shoulder with Medjugorje visionary, Ivanka, when Our Lady appeared to her during her annual apparition on June 25, 1989. Our Lady said:

June 25, 1989

> **"Pray because you are in great temptation and danger because the world and material goods lead you into slavery. satan is active in this plan…"**

Our Lady is the Moses of our time. She has come to lead us out of Egypt, slavery, bondage, away from the lies, and onto the path of truth. Has satan Pulled Another One on You?, gives a big dose of truth. It gives you the path to follow to begin the fight to crush this serpent's head. The answers to this diabolical problem you are facing will manifest the more you pray, study this book and be proactive. David slayed Goliath by being willing to stand up to him. You also are called to fearlessly stand up to the Goliaths you encounter.

We live in a fallen world, a world that has reached the pinnacle, where an antichrist system is being constructed and is nearly complete. The throne to rule the world has been prepared for the one who will rise to claim his seat. Nothing would have prevented him from claiming this seat, but One stands in his way. The Virgin Mary has been sent by Her Son on a rescue mission to save the world with Her messages from Heaven. The Virgin Mary said on May 2, 2009:

"...Look at the signs of the times..."

How are you going to slay Goliath? The Virgin Mary continues in Her above message:

> **"...Do not permit darkness to envelop you. From the depth of your heart cry out for my Son. His name [Jesus Christ] disperses even the greatest darkness..."**

satan, in the end, will not be successful, in our time, to become the ruler of the world. However, we are still operating under this fully-built satanic system and will continue until Our Lady's Secrets tear it down.* We are in a time of grace when we can change the direction of our lives and begin to get out from underneath this system of lies, but we must find the will to do so. We are in a Biblical moment, a manifestation of the Book of Revelation Chapter 12.

* See page x-xi at the beginning of this book for an explanation of the Ten Secrets given to the visionaries of Medjugorje by the Virgin Mary.

It is true that there are many factors that complicate simply getting children off dangerous drugs: divorce and broken families, the amount of violence and immorality children are exposed to on television, the violent video games that children play, the indoctrination going on in the schools, the constant fear and insecurity being fed to the public by the mass media, the spirit of consumerism and materialism that tear down true values, the consumption of social media, the absence of God in our culture, the weakness of the Church, the lack of leadership of the majority of bishops and pastors, regardless of what denomination they are from, and the list goes on and on. But a great many of these could be managed better by simply getting your kids out of pagan-run, antichrist schools and getting more control over your children's lives.

It has been amazing to see the impact the coronavirus pandemic has had on the home-school movement. There has been an explosion of growth, a seismic shift. The number of U.S. children being homeschooled today has **doubled since the start of the pandemic, from roughly 2.5 to five million!** That represents **11% of households nationwide that are now homeschooling their children.** Homeschooling was forced upon school-aged children because of coronavirus, and many parents were thrust out of their comfort zones, having to take on themselves the responsibility of their children's education. But for millions, it was an eye-opening experience. **When schools began to open again, a whopping 40% of parents made a permanent switch to continue homeschooling, rather than send their children back to school.** There are many reasons cited for this change of direction in their lives. Many parents discovered that they liked teaching their children. There was more family time, less time in the car shuttling their kids back and forth to school and school activities, and many of their children had more success at home than in a school setting, etc. Many parents became alarmed in discovering, for the first time, how much indoctrination their children were being exposed to—anti-God, anti-American, anti-family and many other leftist agendas. Even Christian schools have many things that are against your children's faith. Still others, troubled by the violence in schools, the increase in school shootings, the exposure to immorality, drugs, etc., found that their children were safer at home being schooled. Others found homeschooling eased the family's financial burden. Two and a half million families changed the direction of their lives almost instantaneously. It is just as C.S. Lewis said:

> *"We all want progress. But progress means getting nearer to the place you want to be and if you have taken a wrong turn, then to go forward does not get you any nearer. If you are on the wrong road, progress means doing an about-turn and walking back to the right*

road; and in that case, the man who turns back soonest is the most progressive man. We have all seen this when we do arithmetic. When I have started a sum the wrong way, the sooner I admit this and go back and start over again, the faster I shall get on. There is nothing progressive about being pigheaded and refusing to admit a mistake. And I think if you look at the present state of the world, it is pretty plain that mankind has been making some big mistakes. We are on the wrong road. And if that is so, we must go back. Going back is the quickest way on." [200]

C.S. Lewis, Mere Christianity

Homeschooling is a step in the right direction, but it is still not the best answer. The best answer we have here, at the Caritas Community—a one-room schoolhouse. It is the far superior answer. We are in our 27th year with our school, teaching skills and common sense that give children the ability to do <u>any</u>thing they set their minds to do, from everything agrarian, to welding, carpentry, excavation, construction, pottery, graphic design, printing, mechanics and home industry skills, etc., the list goes on and on. You can copy our one-room schoolhouse by starting a neighborhood school, going back to one-room schoolhouses. That is a necessary step for the coming societal change.

Individuals and neighborhood groups or church groups can come to Caritas and visit the Community's one-room schoolhouse and be mentored on the how's and what's of how to start. The simplest thing to do is to schedule a day or two with a group you organize to see and learn what steps to take. One other positive result of the coronavirus is that it has given people more freedom to think out of the box. While I do not agree with the fearmongering that has constantly surrounded everything about the pandemic, it can be useful in moving people towards the idea of smaller schools.

Getting back to nature, to God's Creation, can be an immediate decision that everyone should act upon, because everyone is in need of the renewal that nature brings man. But, for those who are seeking healing for their children in a more natural way, this is one place to start, the first step to take. It costs little or even no money and will bring positive changes. **Again, we caution you not to pull your child or yourself off any medication as an immediate destabilizing of the child's or your own system can be dangerous. It must happen gradually in a weaning process. Find a doctor who is willing to work with you. A doctor's assistance is preferable as withdrawal symptoms can be severe. But do take action to begin the process of getting off these mind-altering medications.**

One other area that came up in our research, that is showing positive results in the process of healing those who have been on psychotropic drugs and diagnosed falsely with ADD or ADHD, is in the treatment of trauma—both physical and emotional trauma. It may be a recent trauma or a trauma that happened even decades ago. Trauma includes a family that has gone through a divorce, the loss of a parent, child abuse, and other destabilizing events that occurred in a child's life. This is an area of study that is fairly new, but as mentioned, showing promise in helping people find healing.

Another area that is essential in the healing process is changing one's diet, eating more organic and natural foods and removing processed foods, white flour and sugar, etc., as much as possible from your child's diet. Research is showing that this alone has changed, if not completely eliminated, a child's "ADD symptoms." Both of these topics were too large of subjects to tackle in this book but we mention them here so that you can begin your own research. People want an easy and fast fix which is why popping pills became so popular. But God requires metanoia, which is a change in mentality, conversion, forgiveness and prayer to lead us towards healing.

While you may feel overwhelmed from all that you have read in Has satan Pulled Another One on You?, and the decisions you are facing may feel daunting, we end with Our Lady's words that are full of encouragement:

December 25, 2018

> **"...little children, full of trust and without looking back and without fear, completely surrender your hearts to Him [Jesus]...Do not be afraid to believe in His love and mercy, because His love is stronger than every one of your weaknesses and fears. Therefore, my children, full of love in your hearts, trust in Jesus and say your 'yes' to Him..."**

THIS SECTION IS NOT TO BE VIEWED UNTIL THE BOOK IS READ. YOU WILL CHEAT YOURSELF, IF YOU READ AHEAD, OF THE PROFOUND HOPE YOU WILL NEED AFTER READING THE ENTIRE BOOK. AGAIN, VERY IMPORTANT, DO NOT REVIEW OR READ THIS SECTION UNTIL AFTER READING THE ENTIRE BOOK.

PICTORIAL SECTION

WARNING:

You Are About To Take A Potent Drug With Severe Side Effects.

While you have read about the effects of psychotropic drugs causing suicidal and homicidal ideation*, what you are about to view is strong medicine that will give you inclinations and strong thoughts to destroy the path you have walked with the culture of death. The world's path is self-destruction and

* As stated previously, but as a reminder, suicidal ideation, often called suicidal thoughts or ideas, is a broad term used to describe a range of contemplations, wishes, and preoccupations with death and suicide. Homicidal ideation is the mental envisioning and planning of a homicide.

murderous. Anyone can see that the world's way to live is anti-life. Therefore, you are called to destroy, in you, the world's deceptions with thoughts that will be prompted by what you are about to see in the following Pictorial Section to experience the joy of life. Just as psychotropic drugs can induce suicidal and homicidal thoughts to the point of leading one to even create elaborate detailed schemes that could lead one to actually fulfill those actions, these pictures have the power to give you thoughts of a new way of life so that the old way of life dies within you.

Do not skim through this Pictorial Section. Say a little prayer before you review these pictures and captions. Go through them very slowly, pause and study each picture individually. Each is a story that will speak to you because the pictures are life and therefore, are alive. It is said, a picture paints a thousand words. Contemplate them and you will experience a thousand thoughts about changing your future. It cannot be done by individual families, but will be achieved by small communities. All that you will see is the fruit of the classroom of a one-room schoolhouse, a small Community foundationed on Philippians 2:2: ***"Then make my joy complete by being like-minded, having the same love, being one in spirit and of one mind."*** This medicine you are about to read is dreamy, but it is not a pharmaceutical-induced illusion. It is real. This little Community in Alabama changes people around the world, reaching out to over 130 countries who are following and adopting this "Way of Life in a New Time."

Recommended:

The book, The Corona Vision, about the future of small communities is a must read. See the order form in the back of this book to order. In order to help you to connect with those in your area, a website/network, **coronavision.net,** is being created to help you find others close to you that are like-minded to birth a small community to start dialoguing and have meetings. It will be set up for the purpose to begin meeting with those who wish to begin a new way of life in a new time. Call Caritas of Birmingham for further information and for the release of this information, 205-672-2000.

Pictorial Section

Everything you will see in the following pages comes from the vision and philosophy of a Friend of Medjugorje through following the messages of the Virgin Mary. This is what he foundationed this little community upon, creating a witness that has had a large impact on people across the globe. The captions give you his guidance.

Cell phones in your hands develop no skills. But a sander in your hand can finish off a molded angel in our pottery shop.

One of the babies in the Community banging rocks. A little one-year-old is developing apprenticeship skills, banging rocks literally into sand, copying what she sees the older children do. Every child who has grown up here (at Caritas) has smashed their finger. They cry, their fingernail turns black, and they go back the next day to bang rocks again. We call it "risk play." They learn two things:

1. How to work, pounding rocks to sand.
2. How to be safe, so you don't smash your finger again.

From these lessons they have less injuries later in life.

Two Community children learning how to handle a knife. Yes, thes are one and two-year-old's playing with sharp knives. We train them how to do it and how to be safe, cutting away fr your fingers and body, not towards them. Whi sometimes they get cut, again, it is a part of "ris play," and a cut teaches them how not to get cu again.

'o people carrying two heavy five-gallon buckets of feed is not bal-
ed. These three girls are carrying two buckets of feed together. La-
is the best classroom and goes hand in hand with apprenticeship.
light years ahead of today's educational system, which stymies the
acity of youth to achieve their highest potential. Through common
se, simple things are learned by just working. Good work ethic is
of the most important virtues for youth to acquire. Work is conso-
on. Consolation gives self-esteem and brings a joyous heart. One
is given a good work ethic will always be able to eat in the future
different world that is being birthed in your midst. A Harvard
earch study that followed a group of children through adulthood
r a 40 year period, found that the happiest adults were those who
'ned from an early age how to work.

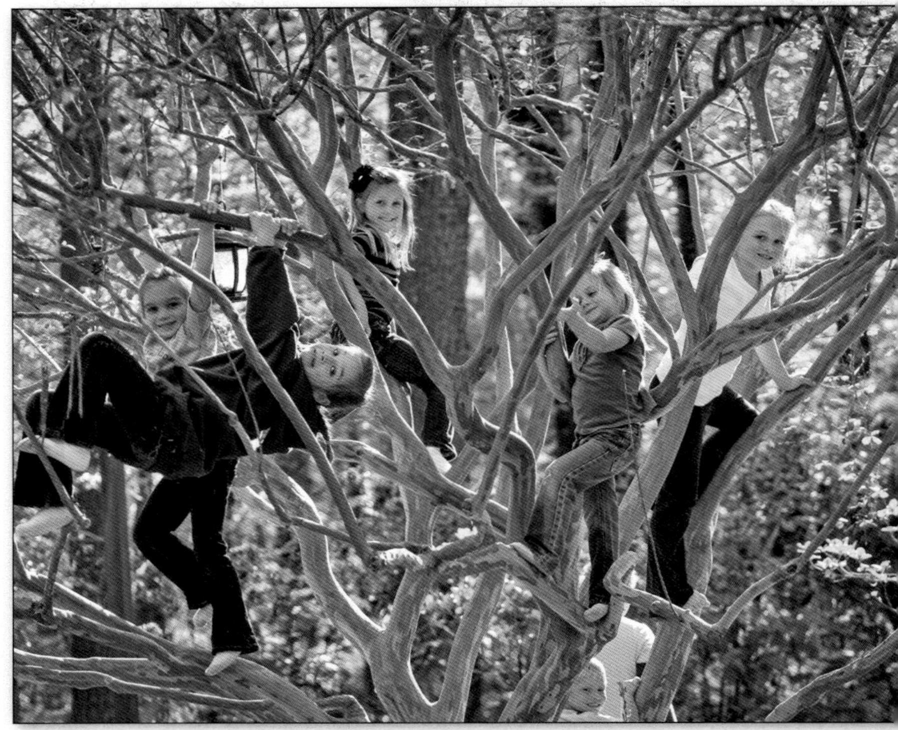

God's monkey bars. God didn't make kids to sit behind a desk for a large part of the day. God made them with energy and that energy is expended through physical activity throughout the day. In Finland, on an average school day, students take a 15-minute break of free play aft every 45 minutes of instruction, making them more attentive in their le sons. Not allowing kids to expend their energy is a reason to dope the down, making them lethargic, even homicidal and suicidal. This is not a sin. It is a mortal sin, because millions of youth are fed pills that pha maceutical CEOs, as well as many of their employees, know that warn of the side effects that come from these diabolic chemicals must be included on the description labels of these drugs. These side effects inclu suicidal and homicidal ideation, meaning a percentage of those who ta these drugs are filled with thoughts to commit suicide and murder. It the reason we have mass shootings in schools and other locations.

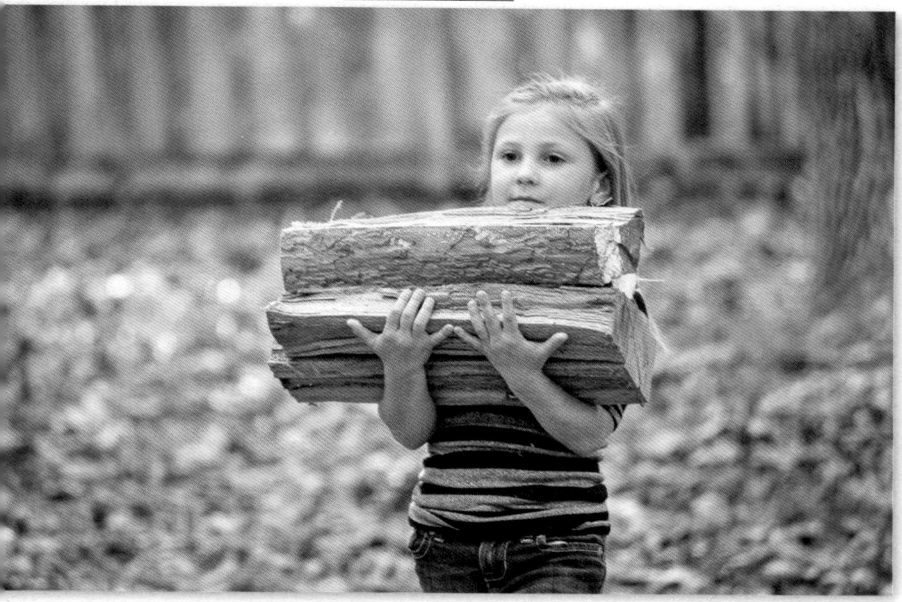

en a four-year-old carrying firewood builds self-worth and gives the child ification of self-confidence in the contribution that they make towards ac- plishing a task.

ge bales to feed our animals become a romping place for kids. "Risk play" cause a broken arm, but it will teach a child how not to break his arm a nd time.

Kids need dirt on them. Let them play in it anytime they want. A 2016 study of the Am showed that Amish communit are immune to many kinds of illnesses and diseases. The Am often walk barefoot, even arou the dairy, sometimes even step ping on cow patties. Don't thi that's bad. Exposure to the th of the earth often give the bod stronger imm system. It's God's progra ming. See be the picture o Amish girl ar the research shows the aft mud and bein around farm animals has their health.

(AP Photo/ Scott R. Galvin)

Recent research on the Amish has revealed that farm life reduces the risk of asthma. Even while their children play barefoot in dairy barns and in farm fields, pets are not allowed inside their homes. Findings show that exposure to microbes found on farms may be boosting Amish children's disease-fightir immune system. Studies are also finding health benefits for those who walk barefoot outside, known as "earthing" (physically connecting your body with earth). Benefits include preventing insomnia, reducing pain and inflammatio improving mental well-being and heart health, and promoting good eyesight.

ned up: agrarian children's wholesome mischief is not the mischief of
-agrarian youth raised in the unwholesome city. THEY DID NOT KNOW
ULTS WERE WATCHING.

alizing they got caught on camera.

We teach our children in our one-room schoolhouse to love everybody. We a not politically correct. Political correctness says kids shouldn't play cowboys and Indians. Today the falsification of what racism is said to be is warping the mentalities of children. Our children play cowboys "and" Indians and we do r apologize for it. Not only is it fun, but it teaches them:

1. To stand against the political agendas that want to rewrite our nation's histo
2. The history and the way of life of a people who lived before us on this lan some who were noble, and some who were not so noble, but both exampl serve to teach valuable lessons to our children.

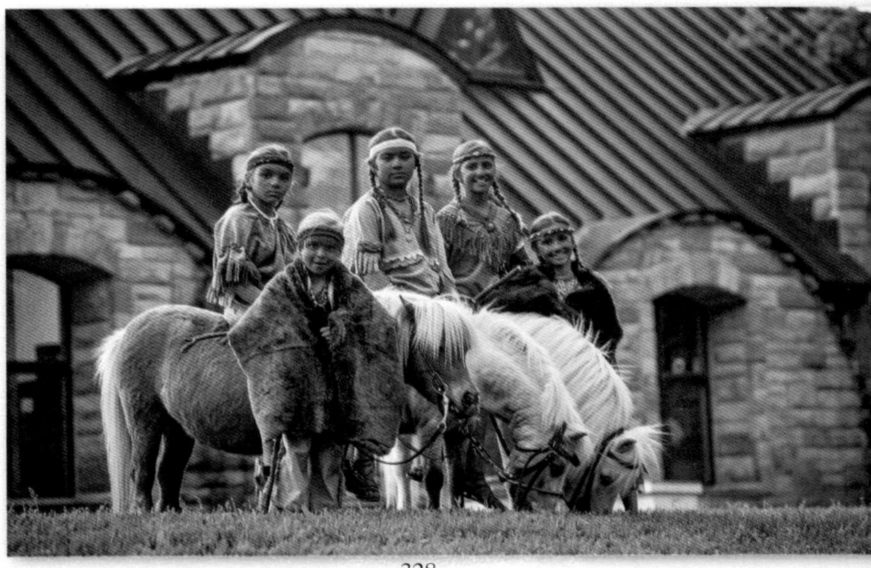

Passing on skills through a one-room schoolhouse, the wigwam behind our little Indian girls was made by their own hands, made on our sawmill, as a school project to show the Community how the clever Indians, in the past with their skills, lived off the land.

The Community sits high up on beams with little kids on parent's laps while praying together and blessing the Community's construction project. Notice the eight-year-old girl going down the ladder carrying a baby. Do you think this is dangerous? Should this not be allowed? Cell phones are dangerous. They destroy the hearts and minds of children. Our children are learning how to navigate their real world, rather than an illusionary world navigated by electronics. Taking cues from their parents and adults around them, they rn not to be afraid of challenges, as seen in this picture, that almost everyone uld label dangerously risky. However, going to the cattle facility schools is far ore dangerous. The youth grow in incredible confidence when obstacles are st overcome by overcoming fears and other negative mentalities. They learn rough experiences and developing skills how to be safe. We do not have TVs, l phones or computers in our homes. Our Lady's way of life teaches to "live e," not "watch" other people live life on TV.

What are they doing? Catching bees of course. N protective gear. In front of hive of hundreds of bees. J a mason jar and their hand No worries about getting stung. Their only desire is t see how many bees they ca catch in their jar. What is th point? The youth of today are raised with electronics. Which is more damaging, playing in front of a beehiv or being in front of a violen computer game? (The bees outside of the jars are circle in yellow.)

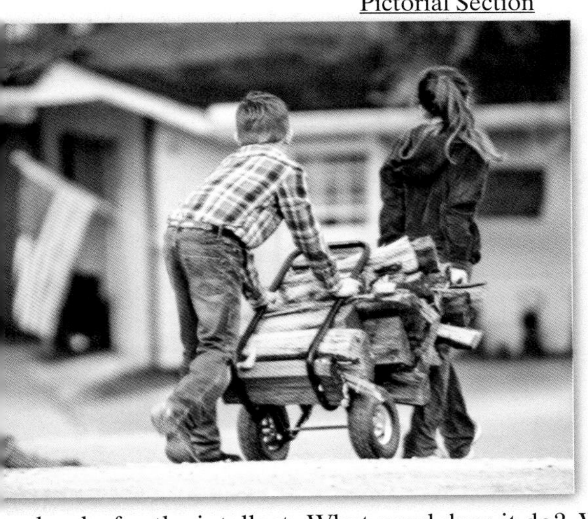

With sweat, this load of wood is split in the heat of the summer and stacked at the one-room schoolhouse. There is no grumbling because there is only a wood stove to heat the school. Purposely, there are no heaters to teach the lessons of life to learn to provide for themselves. The school systems today, first through twelfth grades, only teach ›m books for the intellect. What good does it do? We have millions of youth ıo have no life skills. If graded on life skills alone, they would receive an F-.

:arting a e on a cold ɔrning in ɛ one-room ıoolhouse. ıbor brings y into one's ture.

Life in the one-room schoolhouse. Ponies like to warm up after a cold night. Come on in for the Pledge of Allegiance to the Flag!

What's wrong with you. Stop yelling.

Don't complain! It was in the sta-ble in Bethlehem!

Most of the time it's beautiful in the school, but…sometimes uh oh! Notice th student's coats are still on while the woodstove heats up the school. This helps the youth to grow up "rugged." Today, youth grow up too convenienced and so The future world conditions that are coming are not going to be comfortable.

Our Lady of Victory's Little Schoolhouse—Beloved by the thousands who have visited. The future school system is micro, not mega. Our youth need no college Any occupation can be learned, side by side, through apprenticeship, even doctors, engineers, pilots, etc. First through twelfth grade, teaches them everything they need in life through this little schoolhouse. Anyone can visit anytime. The first day of school is a profound moment for those who come and experience it. Call 205-672-2000 for the date, sometime in September.

There are many "rites of passage" in Community life that come along at different ages and stages of life. One that comes early on is to tackle climbing the tall iron fence that surrounds the Pine Tree in the Field where the Community gathers to pray each day. Regarding our prayer, the adults pray while the children play, bathed in the witness of prayer. As the children grow older, they begin on their own to join us in prayer. While the little ones get a free ride and are placed at the top of the fence by a dad or another adult, the three and four-year-old's have to figure out the technique of how to shimmy up the narrow spindles, haul themselves over the pointy kes, while turning themselves around to finally have a seat up at the top witht falling or spiking themselves. nay take several months, but ıen they finally master the ll, they are proud to be among ꞓ ranks of all the older kids ıo coached and cheered them victory.

ꞓs they conquer the physics balance, suddenly they turn o dare devils commanding an dience's attention. Watch out y, this is real "risk play!" ☺

Do you think it's easy holding onto a slippery piglet? Try it sometime! God ma little people to be with baby animals. There is nothing sweeter and more fun to watch. It is not cruel. What pigs do to each other is cruel. In the fourth picture o the next page, they both have their tongues out!

A newly born calf is surrounded by curious eyes, while mama cow eyes the children. Our children have seen many animals being born: calves, colts, fawns, rabbits, puppies, kittens and little chicks pecking their way out of their shells. And on the other side, they have seen many animals die. Some from old age, some through a tragedy of life. They learn the cycle of life and death, the joy o receiving and the sorrow of letting go; the miracle of birth, and the meaning of Genesis 3:19: ***"For dust you are, and to dust you shall return."***

How do you get down once you are up? Well, there is more than one way to do Notice upside-down Scapulars. Every child is taught to never leave home without their Scapular.* And while the older girls hang like monkeys off the bar, the little one with pig tails looks on with envy dreaming of being able to do that one day he self. Also, going barefoot is very healthy for your immune system (as you read abou the Amish girl with her cow on page 326), even going barefoot in the winter. They kno when to put their shoes on when they get too cold because God gave the sensatio of numbness and common sense. It is the same with coats.

* Many Catholics wear a Scapular. In fact, those who are devoted to the wearing of the Brown Sc ular rarely if ever take it off. It comes with a Heavenly promise that is inscribed upon it: *"Who ever dies 'wearing' this Scapular will not suffer eternal fire."* On the other side: *"Behold the Sign Salvation."* It is not a lucky charm or item of superstition, but the wearing of it is an outward si of faith that God and Our Lady will always move the hearts to deeper conversion who wear th Scapular, and thereby, that soul will escape the eternal fire.

areback, no bridle, on a bucking pony—and off she goes. "You have to get
ck on the horse that threw you," is not just about horses, but is a way of life in
nfronting your failures by not giving up, but trying again.

Horses Are Therapy

The best way for kids to learn to ride a horse is to give them ponies. From the they will learn almost everything needed to know when they begin riding hors The children in the Community can break and train horses. Horses are mystica animals made for man and man for horses. They are God's invention for a car and truck for the agrarian life. These beautiful creatures are very good for the mental health of youth. The greatest joy with horses is when children in multi families in a Community can train and ride many horses together.

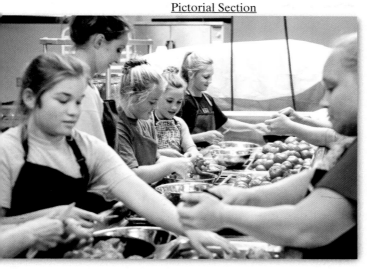

From the picking, to the processing, to the canning—the old adage is true—"Many hands make light work." It is a supreme joy for youth to

k in harmony with adults, side by side, in peace building your future togeth-
The youth grow up with traditions that often follow the seasons of planting
ing), mainte-
ce (summer),
vest (fall) and
(winter). A
of work, a lot
un, and a lot
omato jars
op open to
oy throughout
year.

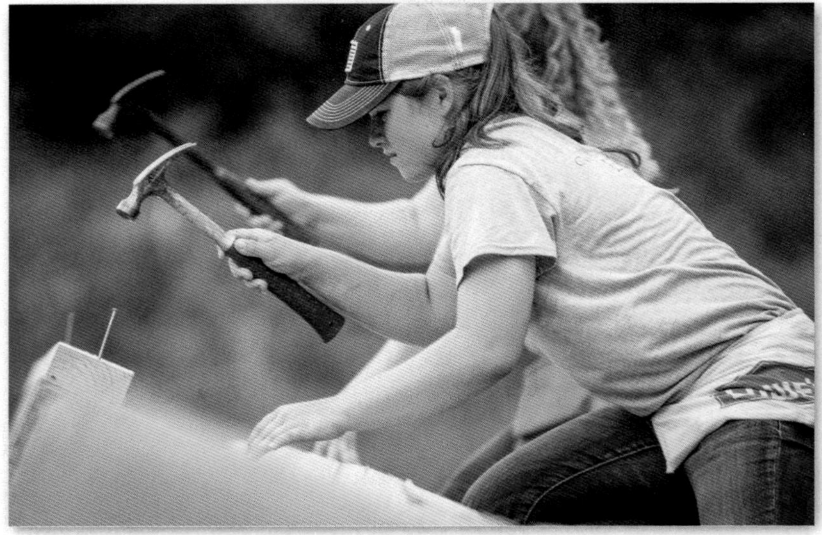

The world is on fire with hatred. So many of our Sacred Institutions are bein destroyed from the inside out. Yet, Our Lady says to build even in the face of such destruction. She says, **"...Today is the day of Peace, but throughout the whole world there is much lack of peace. Therefore, I call you to build up a ne world of Peace together with me, by means of prayer..."** December 25, 1992. Our youth participate in harvesting our own wood, processing it on a sawmill, cutti it to size, and building with it from actual buildings to furniture, to handmade Christmas gifts of quality craftsmanship. With prayer, the life breeds strong youth in mind, body and spirit. And they have the opportunity to expand thei creative gifts in any direction they choose.

Our children don't sing, "Rain, rain go away, come again some other day, little children want to play." Our kids, when they see it rainin run outside shrieking and laughing as they become drenched by a spring/summer/fall shower and sometimes on a mild winter day. makes more laundry for m on those days, but life is to lived, regardless of what th weather forecast gives you

Everything started in the Garden of Eden. There is something holy in getting your hands in the dirt and if given the opportunity, kids love growing things, just as they love raising animals, exploring God's creation, and being part of a bigger picture. Children are not islands and of themselves. They take their cues from their parents and Community lults around them, who all ıve positive attitudes with negativity. God wants always to have gratitude ıether we are in the "mud" the "stars." If parents mplain, that gardening whatever task at hand is hard, or that they would ıch rather be shopping or ecking their social media, n't be surprised that ur children will have the ne negative attitudes. ritas children are raised derstanding it is a great ssing to cooperate with d in His Creation and see how much bounty nes from a single seed. rd work is satisfying to heart and soul when it omplishes great things.

There are not a lot of youth today who would willingly process their own foo
Three or four times a year, the one-room schoolhouse kids of Our Lady of Vic
tory's Little Schoolhouse tackle this job alongside moms and dads and the sing
adults of the Community, sometimes processing 300-400 chickens in a day. The
only thing the children ask is not to have chicken for dinner that night. ☺

. one-room schoolhouse opens the door of possibility and opportunity to learn atever a child wants. One school year all our students studied how to craft l bows as the Indians made them. During one practice shoot, to the surprise l delight of everyone, Joshua's arrow snagged a bird out of the air!

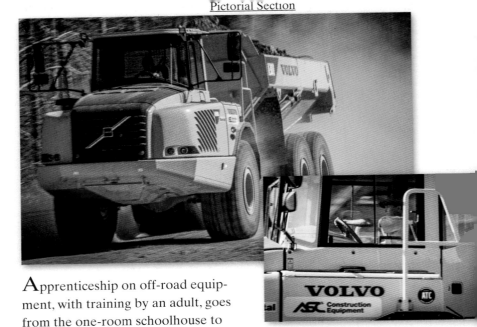

Apprenticeship on off-road equipment, with training by an adult, goes from the one-room schoolhouse to a nine-year-old driving and hauling a full load earth-moving truck weighing 112,568 pounds by himself. You can barely see him over the steering wheel. It moves dirt like a freight train. For the youth, it is exhilarating. Learning to operate all kinds of equipment "is a classroom" in and of itself where skills are learned that will be used for a lifetime.

Up before the sun, working under a hot, humid sun until sundown, heaving 5 pound bales of hay out of freshly cut fields, backbreaking work, with only a sm team of youth is possible because they feel their life has purpose and contribu to a way of life that they love.

ıding a hard day's work gives consolation in knowing what was achieved with ›'s labor: not for money, but for beef, milk, cheese and hay for their horses. It ngs joy seeing the fruit of one's labor. The Lord says in Philippians 2:2:

'Make my joy complete: be of the same mind, having the same love, being n full accord and of one mind."

Give a child a toy and while it may make them happy for a moment, a Friend Medjugorje has always said, "The best toy you can give a child is another child. What makes the water hydrant so fun is that every child is having fun which on multiplies the fun. Today's youth rarely experience euphoric innocent fun anymore. Technology is not fun, it is programming, it is mental activity, hypnotizin mesmerizing, all-consuming. Give a kid another kid and a waterspout and watc them transform into joy.

For nearly 30 years, Our Lady of Victory's Little Schoolhouse has a theme for the year. The first day of school is an elaborate presentation with Community actors, props, animals and backdrops outside and inside. It is something to behold. People drive and even fly in to experience it. Each year, a Friend of Medjugorje writes the foundation meaning of the theme in words. As of the year 2000, a Friend of Medjugorje has written 22 writings to introduce the new school year themes. Below is a writing for the 2009–2010 School Year. A Friend of Medjugorje began these writings after he had formed the foundation of the school. Wanting to be surprised himself on the first day of the school year, he is given only a few words to avoid giving away the entire theme to him. From there, the Holy Spirit takes over. With so little to go on, it is always amazing how his writings are so dead-on when they are unveiled along with the school opening presentation. The writing then guides the teachers as they unfold the theme throughout the school year. The title of his 2009–2010 School Year writing, **Embrace the Hardship**, is written from the perspective of the Virgin Mary as if She was speaking to the school children. It is included here in Has satan Pulled Another One On You? because it is applicable to the lessons in the book, both for parents and the youth. The following picture section is just more of a life of constant work, play, pray and sleep without captions to help you to contemplate what you can be doing to start a one-room schoolhouse in your garage, on your block, in your neighborhood, etc.

Embrace the Hardship

It is I. I, Who take you on the path of hardship. I rode this path not just pregnant, but while in labor. It was God who sent Joseph and I to Bethlehem. I did not hesitate with a flood of thoughts as to why this was to be. I simply embraced the hardship and I followed. It is why I lead you today. Good followers make good leaders.

Today, everyone's desire is always the easy way. Enjoy oneself. For you, I desire you to stop and think. Why does God require for those who are closest to Him to experience struggles? My life, His Son's life, His greatest friends' lives were great struggles and hardships. He does not spare one from walking this path.

It is strange to man's way of thinking that to the degree God commissions a mission, it is paralleled to the degree in hardship. The only way to fulfill your mission is to embrace the hard things required to fulfill your mission. I tell you, mine was difficult, very hard and bitter. Today's man no longer can understand this principle of God, in the way He forms and desires to purify you through these trials. Did I not tell you, "Even today God is testing you," when rain was damaging the whole year's harvest of grapes?* Parents, you today harm your children by feathering their ways, shielding struggles

* Our Lady gave a message in Medjugorje on October 11, 1984, in which She revealed to the villagers that God was testing them through a long rain during the middle of the reaping season which caused a great deal of damage to the crops. Our Lady said:

> **"Dear children, thank you for dedicating all your hard work to God even now when He is testing you through the grapes you are picking. Be assured, dear children, that He loves you and, therefore, He tests you. You just always offer up all your burdens to God and do not be anxious. Thank you for having responded to my call."**

out of their lives, making their lives a constant comfort with little demands except to enjoy themselves. I am warning you, my little children, this is a great harm to you and the ruination of many souls who will lose Eternal Life. I tell you to bear hardship, help one another, love and help those you wish not to. It was a bitter hardship being next to Judas. Yet, God required this of me, what more so from you? Judas' failure began with the minor avoidance of doing things that were hard. His parents demanded little from him and, therefore, had low expectations of him which he, in turn, had low expectations for himself. He was spoiled, incapable of even the simplest things of daily making up his own bed and helping with the simplest of chores.* I tell you, it is little things, little steps of avoiding which leads down the path of an unhappy life of low expectations of yourself – which leads to the loss of Eternal Life. God's expectations for you is to perform perfectly your state in life.

* Italian mystic, Maria Valtorta, who had visions of the life of Christ in the 1940s, was given insights into the lives of the apostles and disciples of Jesus. She described Judas Iscariot as spoiled and indulged as a child by his father. Her visions make up 10 volumes entitled, The Gospel as Revealed to Me, formerly known as The Poem of the Man-God.

I tell you, as I did, not only to embrace the hard things, but in every act throughout your day, prefer the hard things. You will experience joy and the fulfillment of high self-esteem, whereas avoidance of the hard things is mostly rooted in selfishness and little esteem about yourself. It is why you feel better when you do something for someone else, preferring their needs before your own.

My little children, the only path to build a foundation of peace and joy is to:

"Embrace the Struggle!" Do the Hard Thing.

Our Lady Through the Words
of a Friend of Medjugorje
September 12, 2009

Engineering bridges to see them destroyed. School kids, a given only the basics, designed and engineered their own br es and then watched as more and more weight was added to see how much weigl their bridge could hold until it broke. They were on pins and needles, hands clinc to their chins, as each weight was added underneath the bridge. This is engineeri at its best. The winner's prize for their bridge holding the most weight? JOY!

And the winner is…Faith. Her bridge held **218 pounds** before it broke!!

A Friend of Medjugorje has always said: *"Apprenticeship will naturally motivate youth to acquire skills. Skills will naturally require the learning of the 3 'Rs:' 'reading, 'riting, 'rithmetic. With apprenticeship and the 3 'Rs,' there is nothing you cannot do."*

These engineered bridges are just the tip of the iceberg regarding the scope of what these kids are capable of doing. From the very beginning of their lives, they are placed in an environment of learning by observing and doing.

Endnotes

CHAPTER 1

1. Louie Giglio, Don't Give the Enemy a Seat at Your Table: Taking Control of Your Thoughts and Fears in the Middle of the Battle, (Nashville: Thomas Nelson Publisher, 2021).

CHAPTER 2

2. Fred A. Baughman Jr., MD & Craig Hovey, *The ADHD Fraud: How Psychiatry Makes "Patients" of Normal Children*, (Bloomington: Trafford Publishing, 2006), p. 22.
3. *The Rise and Fall of AD(H)D, Testimony before U.S. House subcommittee on "Use of Behavioral Drugs in Schools, chaired by Representative Peter Hoekstra,* (September 29, 2000), (Fred A. Baughman, Jr., M.D.)
4. Ibid.
5. Fred A. Baughman Jr., MD & Craig Hovey, *The ADHD Fraud: How Psychiatry Makes "Patients" of Normal Children*, (Bloomington: Trafford Publishing, 2006).
6. *Diagnostic and Statistical Manual of Mental Disorders, 3rd Edition (DSM-III),* (Washington, DC: American Psychiatric Association, 1980).
7. *The Rise and Fall of AD(H)D, Testimony before U.S. House subcommittee on "Use of Behavioral Drugs in Schools, chaired by Rep. Peter Hoekstra,* (September 29, 2000), (Fred A. Baughman, Jr., M.D.).
8. *Diagnostic and Statistical Manual of Mental Disorders, 3rd Edition (DSM-III),* (Washington, DC: American Psychiatric Association, 1980).
9. Michele Meyer, *Should Your Child Really Be On Ritalin?,* Better Homes and Gardens, (Des Moines: Meredith Corporation, September 2003).
10. *Hearing of the Committee on Government Reform and Oversight*, (July 15, 1996), (Representative Christopher Shays, R-CN).

CHAPTER 3

11. Rowenna Davis, *What does it say about our school system when teachers try to control unruly pupils with drugs?,* May 12, 2010, Daily Mail, https://www.dailymail.co.uk/news/article-1277674/Ritalin-used-control-unruly-pupils.html.
12. *The Rise and Fall of AD(H)D, Testimony before U.S. House subcommittee on "Use of Behavioral Drugs in Schools, chaired by Rep. Peter Hoekstra,* (September 29, 2000) (Fred A. Baughman, Jr., M.D.).
13. Maria Valtorta, *The Poem of the Man-God, Volume Three, #349 "Lessons to the Disciples after the Transfiguration,"* (Isola del Liri: Centro Editoriale Valtortiano 1956).
14. *The Rise and Fall of AD(H)D, Testimony before U.S. House subcommittee on "Use of Behavioral Drugs in Schools, chaired by Rep. Peter Hoekstra,* (September 29, 2000) (Fred A. Baughman, Jr., M.D.).
15. Michele Meyer, *Should Your Child Really Be On Ritalin?,* Better Homes and Gardens, (Des Moines: Meredith Corporation, September 2003.
16. *Opening Remarks at National Institute of Health (NIH) Consensus Conference on ADHD*, (November 16-18, 1998) (S.E. Hyman).
17. *Opening Remarks at National Institute of Health (NIH) Consensus Conference on ADHD*, (November 16-18, 1998) (W.B. Carey).
18. Letter from a father, Caritas of Birmingham archives.
19. Letter from a father, Caritas of Birmingham archives.

CHAPTER 4

20. Rowenna Davis, *What does it say about our school system when teachers try to control unruly pupils with drugs?,* May 12, 2010, Daily Mail, https://www.dailymail.co.uk/news/article-1277674/Ritalin-used-control-unruly-pupils.html.
21. *The Rise and Fall of AD(H)D, Testimony before U.S. House subcommittee on "Use of Behavioral Drugs in Schools, chaired by Rep. Peter Hoekstra,* (September 29, 2000) (Fred A. Baughman, Jr., M.D.).
22. Ibid.
23. *CHADD Jubilant Over Dismissal of California and Texas Class-Action Lawsuits*, Gradda Newsletter, (Spring 2001), https://web.archive.org/web/20050317092350/http://gradda.home.isp-direct.com/sp01chad.html.
24. Ibid.

CHAPTER 5

25. Erin Froehlich, *The Dangers of Ritalin*, The Smart Living Network, (May 20, 2010), https://www.smartlivingnetwork.com/add-adhd/b/the-dangers-of-ritalin/.
26. *The Rise and Fall of AD(H)D, Testimony before U.S. House subcommittee on "Use of Behavioral Drugs in Schools, chaired by Representative Peter Hoekstra,* (September 29, 2000) (Fred A. Baughman, Jr., M.D.).
27. The New American Bible, Revised New Testament, Catholic Edition (Nashville: Thomas Nelson Publishers, 1986).
28. The New American Bible, Catholic Edition (Nashville: Thomas Nelson Publishers, 1970).
29. Letter from Caritas of Birmingham archives.
30. The New American Bible, Revised New Testament, Catholic Edition (Nashville: Thomas Nelson Publishers, 1986).

CHAPTER 6

31. Peter Breggin, M.D. *Psychiatrist Says: More Psychiatry Means More Shootings*, (February 26, 2018), Mad in America, Robert Whitaker, https://www.madinamerica.com/2018/02/more-psychiatry-means-more-shootings/.
32. Leo Hohmann, *Big List of Drug-Induced Killers,* (June 18, 2015), WorldNetDaily (WND), Joseph Farah, https://www.wnd.com/2015/06/big-list-of-drug-induced-killers/.
33. Mark Follman, Gavin Aronsen, Deanna Pan, *A Guide to Mass Shootings in America,* (July 17, 2022), Mother Jones, Monika Bauerlein, https://www.motherjones.com/politics/2012/07/mass-shootings-map/.
34. *Murder Suicide Pact in Texas: Two Teenage Brothers Kill Family, Then Themselves*, (April 5, 2021), SSRI Stories, https://ssristories.org/murder-suicide-pact-in-texas-two-teenage-brothers-kill-family-then-themselves-102-9-karn-news-radio/.
35. Nicole Rojas, *Who is Zephen Xaver? 21-Year-Old Accused of Killing 5 at SunTrust Bank Had 'Fascination With Death'*, (January 24, 2019), https://ssristories.org/who-is-zephen-xaver-21-year-old-accused-of-killing-5-at-suntrust-bank-had-fascination-with-death-newsweek/.
36. https://ssristories.org/troubling-details-uncovered-in-pittsburgh-synagogue-shooting-suspect-robert-bowers-past-kdka-cbs-pittsburgh/.
37. https://ssristories.org/the-latest-sheriff-suspect-may-have-had-mental-illness-whec-news-10/.
38. Leo Hohmann, *Big List of Drug-Induced Killers,* (June 18, 2015), WorldNetDaily (WND), Joseph Farah, https://www.wnd.com/2015/06/big-list-of-drug-induced-killers/.
39. *Troubling Details Uncovered in Pittsburgh Synagogue Shooting Suspect Robert Bowers Past - (KDKA CBS Pittsburgh,* (October 30, 2018), https://thoughtcatalog.com/jeremy-london/2019/09/37-mass-shooters-who-were-on-antidepressants/.
40. Kyle Feldscher, *Las Vegas Shooter Stephen Paddock was Prescribed Anti-Anxiety Drug Months Before Killing,* (October 4, 2017), https://ssristories.org/las-vegas-shooter-stephen-paddock-was-prescribed-anti-anxiety-drug-months-before-killing-the-washington-examiner/.
41. Jerome London, *37 Mass Shooters Who Were on Antidepressants,* (September 11, 2019), Thought Catalog, https://thoughtcatalog.com/jeremy-london/2019/09/37-mass-shooters-who-were-on-antidepressants/.
42. Ibid.
43. Jack Healy, Mike McIntire, Julie Turkewitz, *Oregon Killer's Mother Wrote of Troubled Son and Gun Rights*, (October 5, 2015), The New York Times, https://ssristories.org/oregon-killers-mother-wrote-of-troubled-son-and-gun-rights-the-new-york-times/.
44. https://www.cbsnews.com/news/charleston-shooting-suspect-dylann-roof-drug-suboxone/.
45. Bianca Seidman, *What Was the Drug Dylann Roof Was Holding When Arrested in February?*, (June 22, 2015), CBS News, https://joemiller.us/2018/02/media-ignoring-1-crucial-factor-florida-shooting/.
46. Jerome London, *37 Mass Shooters Who Were on Antidepressants,* (September 11, 2019), Thought Catalog, https://thoughtcatalog.com/jeremy-london/2019/09/37-mass-shooters-who-were-on-antidepressants/.
47. Julie Wood, *FSU Shooter Myron May Left Message: 'I Do Not Want to Die in Vain'* - (NBC News), (November 22, 2014), NBC News, https://ssristories.org/?s=Myron+Deshawn+May.
48. Leo Hohmann, *Big List of Drug-Induced Killers,* (June 18, 2015), WorldNetDaily (WND), Joseph Farah, https://www.wnd.com/2015/06/big-list-of-drug-induced-killers/.
49. Jerome London, *37 Mass Shooters Who Were on Antidepressants,* (September 11, 2019), Thought Catalog, https://thoughtcatalog.com/jeremy-london/2019/09/37-mass-shooters-who-were-on-antidepressants/.
50. Leo Hohmann, *Big List of Drug-Induced Killers,* (June 18, 2015), WorldNetDaily (WND), Joseph Farah, https://www.wnd.com/2015/06/big-list-of-drug-induced-killers/.
51. Ibid.
52. Ibid.
53. Madeleine Baran, *Depression Meds Found in Accent Signage Shooter's Home, Police Say*, (October 8, 2012), MPR News, https://www.mprnews.org/story/2012/10/08/depression-meds-found-in-accent-signage-shooters-home-police-say.
54. Leo Hohmann, *Big List of Drug-Induced Killers,* (June 18, 2015), WorldNetDaily (WND), Joseph Farah, https://www.wnd.com/2015/06/big-list-of-drug-induced-killers/.
55. Jerome London, *37 Mass Shooters Who Were on Antidepressants,* (September 11, 2019), Thought Catalog, https://thoughtcatalog.com/jeremy-london/2019/09/37-mass-shooters-who-were-on-antidepressants/.
56. Ibid.
57. Gina Gallucci, *Middletown Tragedy: Toxicology Report Finds Seven Drugs in Wood's System,* (June 25, 2009 updated March 11, 2016), The Frederick News-Post, https://www.fredericknewspost.com/archive/middletown-tragedy-toxicology-report-finds-seven-drugs-in-woods-system/article_f5919c4a-b4d6-573a-b54f-68b892cc3fdc.html.
58. *Defense: Steward Doesn't Remember Nursing Home Shooting*, (August 9, 2011), WRAL.com, https://ssristories.org/eight-dead-in-nursing-home-jury-spares-death-penalty-due-to-medications/.
59. *School-Related Acts of Violence by Those on or Withdrawing from Psychiatric Drugs*, https://ww1.prweb.com/prfiles/2013/03/15/10534438/31%20School-Related%20Acts%20of%20Violence.pdf.
60. Abbie Boudreau and Scott Zamost, *Girlfriend: Shooter was Taking Cocktail of 3 Drugs*, CNN.com, https://www.cnn.com/2008/CRIME/02/20/shooter.girlfriend/index.html.
61. Mike Adams, *Breaking News: Omaha Shooter Robert Hawkins Had Been 'Treated' for ADHD, Depression*, (December 6, 2007), Organic Consumers Association, https://www.organicconsumers.org/news/breaking-news-omaha-shooter-robert-hawkins-had-been-treated-adhd-depression.
62. *Auvinen Sought to Inflict Maximum Damage in Jokela Shootings - (Helsingin Sanomat),* (November 7, 2007), SSRI Stories, https://ssristories.org/student-kills-8-wounds-10-kills-self-high-school-in-finland/.
63. Karl Turner, *Who was Asa Coon?,* (October 11, 2007), Cleveland.com, https://www.cleveland.com/metro/2007/10/who_was_asa_coon.html.

64. Bob Unruh, *Are Meds to Blame for Cho's Rampage*, (April 23, 2007), WorldNetDaily WND.com, https://www.wnd.com/2007/04/41218/.
65. Jerome London, *37 Mass Shooters Who Were on Antidepressants,* (September 11, 2019), Thought Catalog, https://thoughtcatalog.com/jeremy-london/2019/09/37-mass-shooters-who-were-on-antidepressants/.
66. David Kupelian, *Media Ignoring 1 Crucial Factor in Florida School Shooting*, (February 15, 2018), WorldNetDaily WND.com, https://www.wnd.com/2018/02/media-ignoring-1-crucial-factor-in-florida-school-shooting/.
67. Ibid.
68. *Mamoru Takuma,* Wikipedia.com, https://en.wikipedia.org/wiki/Mamoru_Takuma.
69. Jerome London, *37 Mass Shooters Who Were on Antidepressants,* (September 11, 2019), Thought Catalog, https://thoughtcatalog.com/jeremy-london/2019/09/37-mass-shooters-who-were-on-antidepressants/.
70. Carol A. Clark, *A Brief History of Psychotropic Drugs Prescribed to Mass Murderers*, (January 16, 2013), LA Daily Post.com, https://ladailypost.com/a-brief-history-of-psychotropic-drugs-prescribed-to-mass-murderers/.
71. David Kupelian, *Media Ignoring 1 Crucial Factor in Florida School Shooting*, (February 15, 2018), WorldNetDaily WND.com, https://www.wnd.com/2018/02/media-ignoring-1-crucial-factor-in-florida-school-shooting/.
72. Ibid.
73. Leo Hohmann, *Big List of Drug-Induced Killers,* (June 18, 2015), WorldNetDaily (WND), Joseph Farah, https://www.wnd.com/2015/06/big-list-of-drug-induced-killers/.
74. *Teen Guilty in Mississippi School-Shooting Rampage*, (June 12, 1998), CNN.com, https://ssristories.org/teen-guilty-in-mississippi-school-shooting-rampage-cnn/.
75. James R. Langford, *Teen's Life Full of Contradictions - The 15-Year-Old Who Shot Two Teachers and Then Himself Hinted That He Would Not Be Alive Much Longer,* (October 22, 1995), The Augusta Chronical (GA), https://ssristories.org/15-year-old-shoots-two-teachers-killing-one-then-kills-himself/.
76. Stephen Leith, *Letter to Commissioner, Food and Drug Administration,* SSRI Stories.org, https://ssristories.org/school-teacher-shoots-kills-his-superintendent-at-school/.
77. Leo Hohmann, *Big List of Drug-Induced Killers,* (June 18, 2015), WorldNetDaily (WND), Joseph Farah, https://www.wnd.com/2015/06/big-list-of-drug-induced-killers/.
78. Ibid.
79. *Oakland Elementary School Shooting*, Wikipedia.org, https://en.wikipedia.org/wiki/Oakland_Elementary_School_shooting.
80. Leo Hohmann, *Big List of Drug-Induced Killers,* (June 18, 2015), WorldNetDaily (WND), Joseph Farah, https://www.wnd.com/2015/06/big-list-of-drug-induced-killers/.
81. David Kupelian, *Media Ignoring 1 Crucial Factor in Florida School Shooting*, (February 15, 2018), WorldNetDaily WND.com, https://www.wnd.com/2018/02/media-ignoring-1-crucial-factor-in-florida-school-shooting/.
82. Ibid.
83. Associated Press, *Witness : Andrea Yates Asked if Satan Could Read Her Mind,* (January 13, 2015), FoxNews.com, http://www.foxnews.com/story/2006/07/11/witness-andrea-yates-asked-if-satan-could-read-her-mind.html.
84. David Kupelian, The Giant, Gaping Hole in Sandy Hook Reporting, (January 6, 2013), WorldNetDaily WND.com, https://www.wnd.com/2013/01/the-giant-gaping-hole-in-sandy-hook-reporting/.
85. https://ssristories.org.

CHAPTER 7

86. Peter Breggin, M.D. *Psychiatrist Says: More Psychiatry Means More Shootings*, (February 26, 2018), Mad in America, Robert Whitaker, https://www.madinamerica.com/2018/02/more-psychiatry-means-more-shootings/.
87. David Kupelian, *Media Ignoring 1 Crucial Factor in Florida School Shooting*, (February 15, 2018), WorldNetDaily WND.com, https://www.wnd.com/2018/02/media-ignoring-1-crucial-factor-in-florida-school-shooting/
88. Peter R. Breggin, M.D., *Eric Harris was taking Luvox (a Prozac-like drug) at the time of the Littleton murders*, (April 30, 1999), http://psychrights.org/stories/EricHarris.htm
89. Citizens Commission on Human Rights of Colorado, *The Aurora, Colorado Tragedy - Another Senseless Shooting, Another Psychotropic Drug?,* (July 20, 2012), cchrcolorado.org, https://cchrcolorado.org/the-aurora-colorado-tragedy-another-senseless-shooting-another-psychotropic-drug/

CHAPTER 8

90. Peter R. Breggin, M.D., "Psychiatric Drugs for Children and Youth, A Disaster."
91. Citizens Commission on Human Rights of Colorado, *The Aurora, Colorado Tragedy - Another Senseless Shooting, Another Psychotropic Drug?,* (July 20, 2012), cchrcolorado.org, https://cchrcolorado.org/the-aurora-colorado-tragedy-another-senseless-shooting-another-psychotropic-drug/
92. Ibid.
93. Ibid.
94. Ibid.
95. Ibid.
96. Ibid.
97. Ibid.
98. Citizens Commission on Human Rights Florida, *Antidepressants Are a Prescription for Mass Shootings,* (November 14, 2012), cchrflorida.org, http://www.cchrflorida.org/antidepressants-are-a-prescription-for-mass-shootings
99. Donald J. Trump, *Remarks by President Trump at Whirlpool Corporation Manufacturing Plant*, (August 6, 2020), White House Archives, https://trumpwhitehouse.archives.gov/briefings-statements/remarks-president-trump-whirlpool-corporation-manufacturing-plant/

100. Ibid.
101. Pam Key, *Harvard Professor Pinker: Where Was God When Florida Massacre Happened?,* February 18, 2018, Breitbart News, https://www.breitbart.com/clips/2018/02/18/harvard-professor-pinker-god-florida-massacre-happened/
102. Ibid.

CHAPTER 9

103. Mitch Daniels, *"In Farm Children, I See Virtues That One Sees Too Rarely These Days,"* The Washington Post, (June 11, 2019), The Washington Post, https://www.washingtonpost.com/opinions/thomas-jefferson-was-right-theres-plenty-to-admire-in-agricultural-values/2019/06/11/684ef552-8c5c-11e9-adf3-f70f78c156e8_story.html.
104. Lauren Cassani Davis, *"Horses Can Read Human Facial Expressions,"* The Atlantic Daily, (February 29. 2006), https://www.theatlantic.com/science/archive/2016/02/how-horses-read-human-emotions/471264/.
105. Maria Valtorta, *The Poem of the Man God, Volume One*, (Isola del Liri (Fr): Centro Editoriale Valtortiano, 1954), p. 194.

CHAPTER 10

106. Peter R. Breggin, M.D., *The Hazards of Treating 'Attention-Deficit/Hyperactivity Disorder' with Methylphenidate (Ritalin)*, The Journal of College Student Psychotherapy, Vol. 10(2), (1995), pp. 55-72.
107. *Facts on Veal Calves,* Human Society Veterinary Medical Association, www.hsvma.org/facts_veal_calves
108. Lenore Skenazy and Jonathan Haidt, *The Fragile Generation*, (December 2017), Reason.com, https://reason.com/2017/10/26/the-fragile-generation/
109. Ibid.
110. Ibid.
111. Medjugorje Visionary, Marija Lunetti, told this story during an event in Italy that was held in a soccer stadium. The Medjugorje inner locutionist, Jelena Vlasic was there as well and spoke. A Friend of Medjugorje was present during this event and heard the story directly from her.
112. Lenore Skenazy and Jonathan Haidt, *The Fragile Generation*, (December 2017), Reason.com, https://reason.com/2017/10/26/the-fragile-generation/

CHAPTER 11

113. Citizens Commission on Human Rights International, *37 School Shooters/school Related Violence Committed by Those Under the Influence of Psychiatric Drugs,* CCHR International, The Mental Health Watchdog, https://www.cchrint.org/school-shooters/
114. Martin Peretz, *1895 8th Grade Final Exam: I couldn't Pass it. Could You?*, (November 27, 2010), The New Republic, https://newrepublic.com/article/79470/1895-8th-grade-final-exam-i-couldnt-pass-it-could-you,
115. Joseph P. Harner III and James P. Murphy, Kansas State University, *Planning Cattle Feedlots,/MF-2316 Livestock Systems*, Kansas State University, Department of Biological and Agricultural Engineering, December 2021.
116. Barbara Kent Lawrence, Ed.D., et al., *Dollars and Sense: The Cost Effectiveness of Small Schools*, Knowledge Works Foundation, (2002), https://www.ruraledu.org/user_uploads/file/Dollars_and_Sense.pdf.
117. Msgr. George A. Kelly, *"The Catholic College: Death, Judgment, Resurrection,"* Crisis Magazine, (March, 1, 1987) https://www.crisismagazine.com/1987/the-catholic-college-death-judgment-resurrection.
118. National Center for Education Statistics, *Violence and Discipline Problems in U.S. Schools 1996-1997*, (March 1998), https://nces.ed.gov/pubs98/98030.pdf
119. Barbara Kent Lawrence, Ed.D., et al., *Dollars and Sense: The Cost Effectiveness of Small Schools*, Knowledge Works Foundation, (2002), https://www.ruraledu.org/user_uploads/file/Dollars_and_Sense.pdf.
120. Stuart R. Grauer, Ed.D., *Small Versus Large Schools: The Truth About Equity, Cost and Diversity of Programming in Small and Large Schools,* Community Works Journal: Digital Magazine for Educators, https://magazine.communityworksinstitute.org/small-versus-large-schools-the-truth-about-equity-cost-and-diversity-of-programming-in-small-and-large-schools/
121. Ibid.
122. Barbara Kent Lawrence, Ed.D., et al., *Dollars and Sense: The Cost Effectiveness of Small Schools*, Knowledge Works Foundation, (2002), https://www.ruraledu.org/user_uploads/file/Dollars_and_Sense.pdf ,
123. Susan Marquardt Blystone, *Old School: Reflections of One-Room Schoolhouse Teachers;* (February 17, 2014), Illinois State University, https://news.illinoisstate.edu/2014/02/old-school-reflections-one-room-schoolhouse-teachers/.
124. Ibid.
125. Florence Williams, *The Nature Fix: Why Nature Maeks Us Happier, Healthier and More Creative,* (New York: W.W. Norton & Company, 2017).

CHAPTER 12

126. Florence Williams, *The Nature Fix: Why Nature Makes Us Happier, Healthier and More Creative*, (New York: W.W. Norton & Co., 2017), p. 25.
127. Udoy, Rahman, *The Falcon Cannot Hear the Falconer in "The Second Coming" Poem*, Research Gate, (September 2020), https://www.researchgate.net/publication/344263684_The_Falcon_Cannot_Hear_the_Falconer_in_The_Second_Coming_Poem.
128. Florence Williams, *The Nature Fix: Why Nature Makes Us Happier, Healthier and More Creative*, (New York: W.W. Norton & Co., 2017), p. 78.
129. Ibid., p. 28.
130. Ibid., p. 19.
131. Ibid., p. 22.

132. Ibid., p. 37.
133. Ibid., pp. 39-40.
134. Ibid., p. 41.
135. Ibid., p. 43.
136. Ibid., 44.
137. Ibid., 45.
138. Ibid., p. 59.
139. Ibid., p. 97.
140. Ibid., P. 97.
141. Ibid., P. 115.
142. Ibid., p. 117.
143. Ibid., p. 182.
144. Ibid., p. 144.
145. Ibid., p. 163.
146. Ibid., p. 163.
147. Ibid., p. 171.

CHAPTER 13

148. Louv, Richard, *Last Child in the Woods: Saving Our Children from Nature-Deficit Disorder*, (New York: Workman Publishing Company, 2008), p. 103..
149. Williams, Florence; *The Nature Fix: Why Nature Makes Us Happier, Healthier, and More Creative,* (New York: W.W. Norton & Company, 2017), p. 223.
150. Ibid., p. 234.
151. *SOAR, a Journey to Success,* SOAR, Jonathan Jones, https://soarnc.org/learn-more.
152. ADDitude Editors, *ADHD Statistics: New ADD Facts and Research*, ADDitude Magazine, (July 13, 2022), www.additudemag.com/statistics-of-adhd.
153. Williams, Florence; *The Nature Fix: Why Nature Makes Us Happier, Healthier, and More Creative,* (New York: W.W. Norton & Company, 2017), p. 224.
154. Louv, Richard, *Last Child in the Woods: Saving Our Children from Nature-Deficit Disorder*, (New York: Workman Publishing Company, 2008), p. 102.
155. Ibid., p. 35.
156. Ibid., p. 124.
157. Jaak Panksepp, *"Can PLAY Diminish ADHD and Facilitate the Construction of the Social Brain?"*, Journal of the Canadian Academy of Child and Adolescent Psychiatry, Vol. 16, no. 2, (2007), p. 62.
158. Louv, Richard, *Last Child in the Woods: Saving Our Children from Nature-Deficit Disorder*, (New York: Workman Publishing Company, 2008), p. 109.
159. Williams, Florence; *The Nature Fix: Why Nature Makes Us Happier, Healthier, and More Creative,* (New York: W.W. Norton & Company, 2017), p. 224.
160. Ibid.

CONCLUSION—PART I

161. Jonathan Gornall, *Have millions been taking antidepressants with harmful side-effects for decades - when there's no scientific evidence they do what they claim? Some experts have suspected it for years. Now patients have been left reeling by a ground-breaking study,* DailyMail.co.uk, (July 20, 2022), https://www.dailymail.co.uk/news/article-11033517/Have-millions-taking-antidepressants-harmful-effects-decades-no-reason.html
162. Ibid.
163. Ethan Ennals, *Antidepressants do work, insist top doctors as they hit back at bombshell study which found there was no 'convincing evidence' of a link between low serotonin and mental illness,* DailyMail.co.uk, (July 23, 2022), https://www.dailymail.co.uk/health/article-11042143/Joanne-Moncrieff-University-College-London-disproves-link-low-serotonin-depression.html
164. Ibid.
165. Joe Davies, *Antidepressants DON'T make people any happier, major study claims, DailyMail.co.uk.,* (April 20, 2022), https://www.dailymail.co.uk/health/article-10734869/Antidepressants-DONT-make-people-happier-major-study-claims.html
166. *Read the Prosecutor's Account of Events Before the Michigan School Shooting*, The New York Times, (December 3, 2021), https://www.nytimes.com/2021/12/03/us/michigan-prosecutor-crumbley-charges.html?action=click&module=RelatedLinks&pgtype=Article
167. Thomas Colson, *Prosecutors release troubling drawings by the Oxford shooting suspect, featuring guns and bullets, made on a math worksheet hours before the attack*, Insider.com (December 24, 2021), https://www.insider.com/ethan-crumbley-drawings-math-test-review-2021-12
168. Allan Lengel, *'The Shooting Is Tomorrow, I Have Access To The Gun And Ammo' - Ethan Crumbley's Journal*, DeadlineDetroit.com, (February 24, 2022), https://deadlinedetroit.com/articles/29974/the_shooting_is_tomorrow_i_have_access_to_the_gun_and_ammo_--_ethan_crumbley_s_journal
169. Associated Press, *Parents of teen charged in school shooting to stand trial*, MyNorthwest.com, (February 24, 2022), https://mynorthwest.com/3362706/hearing-to-resume-for-parents-of-school-shooting-suspect/
170. Fred Gardner, *Was Ethan Crumbley on Prozac?*, O'Shaughnesy's Online, (December 4, 2021), https://beyondthc.com/was-ethan-crumbley-on-prozac/
171. Ibid.

172. *Department of Health And Human Services Public Health Service Food and Drug Administration, FDA Psychopharmacologic Drugs Advisory Hearings*, (September 20, 1991) (Bonnie Leitsch), https://ssristories.org/woman-attempts-suicide-on-prozac-2/
173. Julia Jacobo, Morgan Winsor, Jack Date and Pierre Thomas, *Florida suspect said he heard voices telling him to carry out massacre: sources*, ABC News, (February 16, 2018), https://abcnews.go.com/US/florida-school-shooter-methodically-moved-classrooms-execute-victims/story?id=53112929
174. Fred Gardner, *Was Ethan Crumbley on Prozac?*, O'Shaughnesy's Online, (December 4, 2021), https://beyondthc.com/was-ethan-crumbley-on-prozac/
175. Amanda Woods, *Dayton shooter Connor Betts heard menacing voices, talked about 'evil things'"ex,* New York Post, (August 6, 2019), https://nypost.com/2019/08/06/dayton-shooter-connor-betts-heard-menacing-voices-talked-about-evil-things-ex/
176. Phil Stewart and Scott Malone, *U.S. Navy was warned that Washington shooter 'heard voices'*, Reuters, (September 16, 2013), https://www.reuters.com/article/us-usa-navy-shooting/u-s-navy-was-warned-that-washington-shooter-heard-voices-idUSBRE98F0DN20130917
177. Elise Kaplan, *Warehouse shooter called 911, said he heard voices,* Albuquerque Journal, (November 15, 2018), https://www.abqjournal.com/1247081/warehouse-shooter-called-911-said-he-heard-voices.html
178. KUNM News, Police Say Student Reported Hearing 'Voices' Before Shooting, The University of New Mexico KUNM Radio, (February 14, 2019), https://www.kunm.org/local-news/2019-02-14/police-say-student-reported-hearing-voices-before-shooting
179. Corky Siemaszko and Tracy Connor, *Fort Lauderdale Airport Shooting Suspect Esteban Santiago Said He Heard Voices: Officials,* NBC News, (January 7, 2017), https://www.nbcnews.com/news/us-news/fort-lauderdale-airport-shooting-suspect-complained-hearing-voices-officials-n704081
180. Philip Caulfield, *Maryland mall gunman was obsessed with Columbine massacre, posted chilling message to Tumblr seconds before attack: police chief,* New York Daily News, (March 12, 2014), https://www.nydailynews.com/news/national/maryland-mall-gunman-obsessed-columbine-massacre-posted-chilling-message-tumblr-seconds-attack-police-chief-article-1.1719382
181. Jeff Barnard, *School Killer Heard Voices In His Head\Kip Kinkel Appeared To Be A Normal 15-Year-Old Kid, But He Listened To The Angry Voices That He Says Told Him to Kill*, Greensboro News and Record, (November 14, 1999, Updated January 25, 2015), https://greensboro.com/school-killer-heard-voices-in-his-head-kip-kinkel-appeared-to-be-a-normal-15/article_f60f4e45-aae7-5bfd-8f58-33db82efbdba.html
182. Ann O'Neill and Sara Weisfeldt, *Psychiatrist: Holms thought 3-4 times a day about killing*, CNN.com, (June 17, 2015), https://www.cnn.com/2015/06/16/us/james-holmes-theater-shooting-fenton/index.html
183. Sara Jean Green and Vernal Coleman, *Ybarra tells jury voices of God, Columbine shooter compelled him to go on SPU rampage,* Seattle Times Law & Justice, (October 31, 2016), https://www.seattletimes.com/seattle-news/law-justice/ybarra-said-voices-of-god-columbine-shooter-compelled-him-to-go-on-spu-rampage/
184. Eric Levenson, Leyla Santiago and Gregory Lemos, *Nikolas Cruz pleads guilty to murder charges and apologizes for Parkland high school massacre*, CNN.com, (October 21, 2021), https://www.cnn.com/2021/10/20/us/nikolas-cruz-parkland-shooting-guilty/index.html
185. Alex Johnson, *Parkland shooting suspect Nikolas Cruz spoke of 'voices,' says he attempted suicide*, NBC News, (August 6, 2018), https://www.nbcnews.com/news/us-news/parkland-shooting-suspect-nikolas-cruz-spoke-voices-says-he-attempted-n898151
186. Emily Shugerman, *Stephen Paddock 'used to lie in bed screaming and may have been in mental anguish': Police are still searching for a motive in the mass shooting*, Independent.co.uk., (October 6, 2017), https://www.independent.co.uk/news/world/americas/stephen-paddock-mental-health-screaming-bed-claims-last-vegas-shooting-latest-a7987481.html
187. *Department of Health And Human Services Public Health Service Food and Drug Administration, FDA Psychopharmacologic Drugs Advisory Hearings*, (September 20, 1991) (Bonnie Leitsch), https://ssristories.org/woman-attempts-suicide-on-prozac-2/
188. Fred Gardner, *Was Ethan Crumbley on Prozac?*, O'Shaughnesy's Online, (December 4, 2021), https://beyondthc.com/was-ethan-crumbley-on-prozac/
189. Ibid.
190. David Kupelain, *Media ignores 1 crucial factor in Florida school shooting*, WorldNetDaily (WND), (February 15, 2018), https://www.wnd.com/2018/02/media-ignoring-1-crucial-factor-in-florida-school-shooting/
191. Ibid.
192. Annie Reneau, *The suicide rate for kids ages 10-14 nearly tripled in the past decade. Why? And what can we do?*, Upwothy.com., (December 5, 2019), https://www.upworthy.com/the-suicide-rate-for-kids-ages-10-14-nearly-tripled-in-the-past-decade-why-and-what-can-we-do
193. John Read Ph.D., *Are Children and Adolescents Overprescribed Psychiatric Medications?: The psychiatric drugging of our children: A developing international crisis*, Psychology Today, (August 17, 2021), https://www.psychologytoday.com/us/blog/psychiatry-through-the-looking-glass/202108/are-children-and-adolescents-overprescribed
194. Ibid.
195. Ibid.
196. *Personal Injury Market Growth: The Personal Injury Market Continues to Rise Year on Year*, Lawyer Monthly, (2022), https://www.lawyer-monthly.com/2022/02/personal-injury-market-growth-the-personal-injury-market-continues-to-rise-year-on-year/
197. David Abels, *Nationwide Personal Injury Statistics*, Abels & Annes, P.C., https://www.daveabels.com/nationwide-personal-injury-statistics/

CONCLUSION PART II

198. Bessel van der Kolk, T*he Body Keeps the Score: Brain, Mind and Body in the Healing of Trauma*, (New York: Penguin Books, 2015.
199. *Number of Jews at Exodus at Exodus,* Aish.com, (August 17, 2011), https://aish.com/number_of_jews_at_exodus/.
200. C.S. Lewis, *Mere Christianity,* (New York: HarperCollins Publishers, April 21, 2015).

Index

A

Agrarian 122, 128, 131, 188, 204, 205, 313, 327, 338
Agrarian Deficit Disorder 130, 131
Agrarian way of life 116, 117, 180, 251
Amish 326
Amphetamines 23
Ancient Egypt 299–303, 306
Anecdotal 278
Angel of Death 300
Antianxiety drugs 70, 75
antichrist system 307
Antidepressant manufacturers 279
Antidepressants 62, 67, 68, 70, 72, 73, 75, 76, 77, 78, 79, 80, 82, 84, 87, 88, 89, 98, 100, 101, 180, 197, 252, 254, 255, 256, 260, 261, 268, 269, 271
Antipsychotic drugs 72, 74, 79, 82, 96
Apprenticeship 115, 180, 225, 321, 323
Ash Wednesday 64, 105, 108
Asthma 326
Atchley, Paul 212, 214, 215, 216
Atchley, Ruth Ann 213
Attention Deficit Disorder (A.D.D.) 15–20, 37, 48, 130, 242, 253, 314
Attention Deficit Hyperactivity Disorder (A.D.H.D.) 16–21, 29, 30, 33, 35, 36, 38, 46, 48, 55, 56, 69, 70, 72, 101, 130, 233, 236–239, 242–244, 248, 253, 314

B

Bales of hay 346
Barefoot 326, 336
Baughman, Dr. Fred A. 14, 30, 32, 47, 48
The Bedroom of Apparitions 177
Beehive 330
Bees 330
Beethoven 41
Behavioral problems 24, 233
Bennett, Tom 44
Benzodiazepines 62
Bible Verses
- 1 Timothy 6:10 1
- Ephesians 6:12 64
- Genesis 3:19 117, 188
- Isaiah 1:18-20 304
- Luke 17:12 281
- Matthew 6:24 99
- Philippians 2:2 319

Biblical principles 45
Biblical worldview 25
Black box FDA warning 83, 84, 102, 148
Blystone, Susan 176
The Body Keeps the Score 298
Bows & arrows 345
Brain abnormality 15
Brain-disabling 62

Brain diseases 13
Brain malfunction 15
Breggin, M.D., Peter R. 62, 90, 94, 132
Broken arm 325
Bullying 135

C

Canning 339
Carey, W.B. 36
Carpentry 124, 313
St. Catherine of Siena 43
Cattle-handling facilities (Schools) 152, 155, 157, 169, 173, 176, 177, 181, 183, 329
Cell phones 128, 147, 321, 329
Chemical Abnormalities 55
Chickens 344
Child labor laws 122–125
Children and Adults with Attention Deficit/Hyperactivity Disorder (C.H.A.D.D.) 16–17, 21, 47–48, 60
Citizens Commission on Human Rights (C.C.H.R.) 93, 98
Clark, Professor Jane 247
Class action lawsuit 48
Communist Police 138
The Community of Caritas 125, 144, 145, 148, 177, 178, 190, 312, 313, 319, 329
Computer games 330
Computers 329
Consolidation of schools 176
Containerized kids 247
coronavirus 309, 310, 313
The Corona Vision 131, 319
Cortisol 194–196, 209
Council on Scientific Affairs of the American Medical Association 33
Created disorders 29
Creeping gradualism 169
Cross Mountain 141–142
Culture of consumerism 172–173

D

Daniels, Mitch 112
David 307
Declaration of Independence 164
Diet 23, 315
Diller, Lawrence H. 55
Disorders 29–30
Divorce 25
DNA 118
Don't Give the Enemy a Seat at Your Table: Taking Control of Your Thoughts and Fears in the Middle of the Battle 4
Drug free school 24
Drugging behavior 24
Drugging kids 56
Drugging of millions 30
Drugs 8–10, 13, 18, 18–24, 29, 33–37, 37, 42, 45, 46, 51, 52, 66, 73, 74, 77, 84–89, 91, 93,

94, 98, 100, 101, 102, 103, 129, 130, 131, 147, 162, 178, 184, 233, 235, 238, 242, 243, 253, 254, 257, 260, 261, 263, 266, 281, 281–285, 290, 294, 297, 298, 309, 311, 324. *See* Medications
Dumbed down 56, 156

E

Earthing 326
Earth-moving truck 346
Ecstasy 223
Edison, Thomas 41
Egypt 306
Egyptians 299–303
Eighth Grade Final Exam (1895) 153, 155
Einstein, Albert 43
Embrace the Hardship 350
Emotional Trauma 315

F

Fact-checkers 304
Fake News 303
Falcons 198
Family problems 257
Fasting 189–193
Fenton, Dr. Lynne 274
Finland 324
Firewood 325
Food and Drug Administration (FDA) 74, 83, 88, 91, 97, 261, 263, 268, 277–279, 280, 282
Forest baths 210
Forest Therapy Trails 210
Fractal dimensions 222, 223
The Fragile Generation 135, 137, 139, 142
Pope Francis 114
Frankenberger, William 35–36
Free play 143–144, 324
Free-range kids 135
Free to Learn 143

G

Gaming addictions 208
Gardening 343
Garden of Eden 343
Gardner, Fred 260, 261, 269
Giglio, Louie 4
Global pharmaceutical manufacturer 100
God's Creation 208, 231, 251, 314, 343
God the Creator 200, 202–203
Goliath 307
Grauer, Dr. Stuart 169, 171
Grauer School 169
Gray, Peter 143
Gun Control Laws 252

H

Haidt, Jonathan 135, 137
Hartman, Geoffry 231
Hayfield 346
Holmes, Debbie 87
Homeschooling 51, 153, 175, 251, 309–312

Homicidal Ideation (Homicidal thoughts). *See* Side Effects and Symptoms.
Homicides 267, 276, 277, 305, 317
Horses 119–122, 337, 347
Human Development Center at the University of Wisconsin 35–36
Hyman, S.E. 35
Hyperactivity 18, 33, 180

I

Illinois State University 177
Indians 328–329, 345
Institute of Safe Medication 101
Isaiah 304
Israelites 299–303

J

Jars 339
Jones, Jonathan 238–239
St. Joseph 124

K

Knives 322
Kupelian, David 83, 85, 86, 91, 283

L

Last Child in the Woods 232, 246
Laundry 342
Leitsch, Bonnie 261–266, 273, 277, 279
Pope Leo XIII 108
Let Grow 134
Lincoln, Abraham 43
Louv, Richard 232, 246
Lunetti, Marija (Medjugorje Visionary) 31
Lying Voices 303–304

M

Mania. *See* Side effects and symptoms.
Mass Murder 85, 92, 93, 97
Mass produce education 155
Mass production educational facilities 152
Mass shootings 66, 67, 69, 100, 101, 252, 253, 275, 277, 296. *See also* Shootings.
Medical privacy laws 267–268
Medications
- Adderall 19, 29, 139, 253, 275, 277
- Ambien 73, 76, 77
- Amitriptyline 82
- Anafranil 83
- Celexa 80
- Clonazepam 75
- Clonodine 78
- Dexedrine 19
- Effexor 80, 87, 88, 91, 92, 101
- Fanapt 74
- Guanfacine 19
- Lexapro 76
- Luvox 80, 92, 93, 101, 268
- Mirtazapine 74

Paxil 79, 86, 101, 268
Pristiq 101
Prozac 70, 73, 77, 79, 80, 81, 82, 86, 92, 93, 100, 101, 253, 260–265, 269, 273, 275, 277–279
Risperdal 73
Risperidone 72
Ritalin 17, 21, 28, 29, 33, 35, 38, 39, 40, 41, 46–48, 51–52, 54–60, 81, 130, 139, 162, 178, 180, 181, 253, 275, 277
Sertraline 75
Strattera 19
Suboxone 71
Thorazine 82
Trazodone 72, 74, 78, 271
Vyvanse 19, 72
Wellbutrin 72
Xanax 76, 77, 83, 270
Zoloft 75, 79, 81, 268
MedWatch 97
Mental health 90
Mental illness 68, 69, 255, 267, 271, 272, 274
Metanoia 316
Methylphenidate 19
Mind-altering chemicals 68, 284
Mind-altering drugs 62, 65, 71, 257, 265, 284
Mind-altering medications 314
Moncrieff, Professor Joanna 255
Moses 299–303
Mud 326

N

Nash, Ogden 12
National Institute of Mental Health 35
Natural Law 24, 49
The Nature Fix 237, 250
Nature Views 222
Neighborhood school 313
Neurotoxic drugs 62
Neurotoxins 62
NK cells 209–210
NK count 209, 210
Nondrug treatments 298
Normal, Illinois 177

O

One-room schoolhouse 152–153, 173–184, 312–313, 318, 329, 331, 344, 345, 346, 350
Opioids 22, 71
Ottosson, Johan 229–230
Our Lady 5
Our Lady of Victory's Little Schoolhouse 177–181, 332, 344, 349

P

Pandemic 310, 313
Paranoia 274
Parental Neglect 259
Parent Teacher Association (P.T.A.) 167
Park 230
St. Paul the Apostle 56–57
Pay special attention (P.S.A.) 20–21

People for the Ethical Treatment of Animals (P.E.T.A.) 119
Perry, Leon (13 year old) 28
Pharaoh 299–301
Pharmaceutical companies 17, 85, 86, 91, 101, 102, 130, 220, 253, 277
  Ciba-Geigy 16, 17, 21, 29, 47, 60
  Ciba Specialty Chemicals 29
  Eli Lilly 86, 100, 278–279, 285
  GlaxoSmithKline 86
  Novartis 29, 47, 60
  Solvay Pharmaceuticals 92
  Wyeth Pharmaceuticals 88, 91, 92
Pharmaceutical heads 324
Pharmaceutical industry 13, 86
Pharmaceutical manufacturers 85
Physical realm 193
Piglet 334
Pinker, Professor Steven 106
Placebo effect 256
PLOS One 100
Political correctness 328
Ponies 331, 337, 338
Post-traumatic stress disorder (P.T.S.D.) 230
Prescription drugs 96, 103, 265
Prison 221
Profit sickness 15
Promised Land 299–303
Prozac. *See* Medications.
Prozac survivors support group 261
Psychiatric drugs 74, 78, 84, 93, 94, 95, 96, 97, 99, 276
Psychiatric drug warnings 98
Psychiatric hospital 68
Psychiatric medication 68, 69, 70, 270, 293
Psychiatric medicines 293
Psychopharmacologic Drugs Advisory Hearings 261, 263, 277
Psychopharmacology 13
Psychosis 270, 274
Psychotic behavior 263
Psychotic drugs 297, 306. *See* Antipsychotic drugs.
Psychotropic drugs 33–34, 66, 67, 69, 130, 253, 256, 257, 261, 266, 267, 272, 275, 277, 281, 283, 288, 314, 317, 318

R

Racism 328
Rain 342
Rare adverse events 88
Report Card 133–134
Ringholz, Dr. George 87, 88
Risk Play 321, 322, 325, 333
Ritalin. *See* Medications.
Running on Ritalin 55

S

Sawmill 329, 340
Scandinavia 180
Scapular 336
Schizophrenia 270

School massacre 99
School psychologist 57
School shooters 96
School shootings 66, 95, 96, 104, 105, 107, 155, 253. *See also* Shootings.
School writing 349
Sedatives 23, 75
Selective serotonin reuptake inhibitor (S.S.R.I) 254, 256–257, 261, 269
Selective serotonin reuptake Inhibitor (S.S.R.I) 84, 100
Self-esteem 113, 134, 147, 162, 209, 241, 323
Serotonin 254
Shay, Congressman Christopher 23
Sheen, Venerable Archbishop Fulton 160
Shooters 66–80, 67–82, 85, 260, 270–275, 283
  Aguilar, Darion Marcus 272
  Alexis, Aaron 74, 271–272
  Auvinen, Pekka-Eric 78
  Betts, Conner 270
  Bowers, Robert 68
  Carneal, Michael 81
  Castillo, Alvaro Rafael 78
  Cetin, Arcan 70
  Coon, Asa 78
  Crumbley, Ethan 258–261, 269–270
  Cruz, Nikolas 69, 72, 266–267, 275
  Dann, Laurie Wasserman 83
  DeKraai, Scott 75
  Engeldinger, Andrew 74
  Harris, Eric 80, 92–93, 275
  Hawkins, Robert 77
  Hoffman, Jason 80
  Holmes, James 74, 99, 273
  Kazmierczak, Steven 77
  Kelley, Devin 69
  Kinkel, Kip 81, 273
  Klebold, Dylan 80, 268–269
  Lanza, Adam 74, 99
  Leith, Stephen 82
  Lopez, Ivan 73
  May, Myron Deshawn 72
  McDermott, Michael 80
  Melton, Waid Anthony 271
  Mercer, Chris Harper 71
  No name 271
  Paddock, Stephen Craig 69, 70, 275
  Pittman, Christopher 79
  Purdy, Patrick 82
  Reyes, Jose 73
  Roof, Dylann Strom 71
  Saari, Matti 77
  Santiago, Estebon 272–273
  Schell, Donald 86
  Seung-Hui, Cho 78
  Shick, John 75
  Sincino, Toby R. 81
  Sonboly, Ali David 70
  Stewart, Robert Kenneth 76
  Stone, Bradley 72
  Takuma, Mamoru 79
  Towhid, Farbin 67
  Towhid, Farhan 67
  Weise, Jeff 79
  Wesbecker, Joseph T. 82
  Wilson, James 82
  Wood, Christopher Alan 76

Woodham, Luke 81
Xaver, Zephen 67
Ybarra, Aaron 72, 274
Shootings 63–64, 67–82, 95, 270–275, 290
Accent Signage Systems 74
Albuquerque, New Mexico 271
Allen, Texas 67
Arora, Colorado 273
Aurora, Colorado 75, 99
Blacksburg, Virginia 78
Blackville-Hilda High School 81
Broward County, Florida 272
Buffalo, New York 67
Burlington, Washington 70
Carthage, North Carolina 76
Cascade Mall 70
Chelsea High School 82
Cleveland, Ohio 78
Cleveland School 82
Columbine High School (Colorado) 63, 92, 162, 267, 272, 275
Country Music Festival 70
Dayton, Ohio 270
Edgewater Technology 80
El Cajon, California 80
Finland 77
Florida State University 72
Fort Lauderdale International Airport 272
Franklin, Massachusetts 79
Granite Hills High School 80
Greenwood, South Carolina 83
Harris, Eric 268
Heath High School 81
Highland Park, Illinois 67
Hubbard Woods Elementary School 83
Las Vegas, Nevada 70, 97, 275
Louisville, Kentucky 82
Marjory Stoneman Douglas High School 1, 63, 69
Marriotsville, Maryland 272
Maryland 68
Michigan 258
Middletown, Maryland 76
Montgomery County, Pennsylvania 72
Moseley, Snochia 68
Munich Olympia Shopping Centre 70
New Mexico High School 271
Newtown, Connecticut 74
Northern Illinois University 77
Oakland Elementary School 82
Omaha, Nebraska 77
Orange High School 79
Osaka Elementary School 79
Paducah, Kentucky 81
Parkland, Florida 1, 63, 69, 104, 105, 107, 108, 266, 275
Pearl, Mississippi 81
Pine Lake Rehab Center and Nursing Home 76
Pittsburgh, Pennsylvania 68
Red Lake Indian Reservation 79
Roseburg, Oregon 71
Salon Meritage hair salon 75
Sandy Hook Elementary School 63, 74, 99
Seal Beach, California 75
Seattle Pacific University 72, 274
Sebring, Florida 67

South Carolina 71, 97
Sparks Middle School 73
Springfield, Oregon 273
Standard Gravure 82
Stockton, California 82
SuccessTech Academy 78
SunTrust Bank 67
Sutherland Springs, Texas 69, 97
Thurston High School 81, 273
Tree of Life Synagogue 68
Tuusala, Finland 78
Umpqua Community College 71
University of Pittsburgh 75
Uvalde, Texas 67
Virginia Tech 63, 78
Wakefield, Massachusetts 80
Washington D.C. 74, 271
Washington Navy Yard 271
Western Psychiatric Institute 75
Westroads Mall 77
Winnetka, Illinois 83

Shooting video 258

Side effects and symptoms 66, 272, 324
Addiction 98
Aggressive behavior 70, 98
Death 98
Emotional Problems 98
Hearing voices 258, 260, 260–261, 266, 270–275, 271, 272, 276
Homicidal ideation (homicidal thoughts) 66, 75, 83, 84, 88, 91, 95, 97, 98, 102, 147, 253, 260, 274, 281, 285, 317, 317–318, 318, 324
Irrational thoughts 262
Mania 66, 92, 95, 97, 98
Psychosis 66, 92, 98
Seeing demons 258
Suicidal ideation (suicidal thoughts) 66, 71, 83, 84, 98, 101, 102, 131, 253, 260, 263, 280, 281, 285, 317, 317–318, 318, 324
Withdrawal 98, 314

Skenazy, Lenore 134, 135, 137, 142
Slavery 305, 306
Smith, Zack 237–240, 244
Smyth, Dr. Joshua 219–220
Snowflakes 136
SOAR 238–241
Soubirous, St. Bernadette 43
Soundscapes 219
South Korea 208
Spiritual realm 193
SSRI 73, 77, 84, 89, 100
SSRI Stories 89
Stimulant drugs 23, 29, 181
Stimulants 62
Strayer, Dr. David 211, 212
Suicidal 83
Suicidal ideation (suicidal thoughts). *See* Side effects and symptoms.
Suicide 52, 67, 68, 70, 71, 73, 74, 77, 78, 82, 84, 85, 98, 102, 148, 264, 267, 271, 276, 277, 278, 285, 292, 305, 324
Sweatshops 122, 124

T

The Tabernacle of Our Lady's Messages 145, 179, 225
Taylor, Richard 226
Ten Commandments 25, 26
The Ten Secrets of Medjugorje 108, 250, 308
The Gospel as Revealed to Me 31. *See also* The Poem of the Man-God
The mental health watchdog 93
The Nature Fix 194, 208
The Poem of the Man-God 31, 352
Therapy 338
Tomatoes 339
Training horses 119–122
Trauma 230, 231, 315
Tree in the Field of Apparitions 333
Tritt, Travis 252
Trujillo, Cardinal Alfonso López 160
Trump, President Donald J. 102–103, 123

U

Unalienable right 49
United States Constitution 164, 165
University of Kansas 213
University of Utah 211
Unstructured play 144
Unsupervised time 138
U.S. Department of Education 162

V

St. Valentine's Day 64
Valtorta, Maria 31, 124, 352
Van der Kolk, Bessel 298
Veal 133, 135, 136, 140
Vianney, St. John 43
Violent video games 208, 309
Voices. *See* Side effects and symptoms.

W

Washing the dishes 125–126
Water hydrant 348
Waters and Kraus 47
Weaning 314
White supremacist 72
Williams, Florence 194, 208, 216, 218, 223, 226, 231, 237, 239, 244, 250
Wood-burning stove 179, 331, 332
Wordsworth, William 230, 230–231, 231

Y

Yates, Andrea 86, 87, 88
Yeats, William Butler 197, 199

Disclaimer

This book expresses the views, opinions, recommendations, suggestions, conclusions, and interpretations solely of the author. The author is not a medical doctor, nor a medical researcher. The author is not a lawyer. The author is not rendering any medical, legal, or other professional advice. You should consult with your or your child's physician before taking, modifying or stop taking any medication. Since your situation is fact-dependent, you should seek the services of an appropriately licensed legal or medical professional before making any decisions or taking any action after reading this book.

About the Witness

Many who will read these books have been following the writings of a Friend of Medjugorje for years. His original and unique insights into the important events of our day have won credence in hundreds of thousands of hearts around the world, with those affecting others, thereby, touching into the millions. His moral courage in the face of so many leaders caving in to the pressures of a politically correct world is not only refreshing, but, according to tens of thousands of written testimonies over 35 years, has helped to strengthen deeply those who desire to live the fullness of their Christian faith. His insights have repeatedly proven prophetic, having their source in the apparitions of the Virgin Mary in Medjugorje. Deeply and personally influenced by the events surrounding Medjugorje, he gave himself to the prayerful application of the words of the Virgin Mary into his life. He has spoken all over the world on Our Lady's messages and how to put them into everyday life. He came to understand that Our Lady was sent by God to speak to mankind in this time because the dangers man is facing are on a scale unlike any the world has ever known since Noah and the flood. He is not an author. He is a witness of what Our Lady has shown him to testify to—first, by his life—secondly, through the written word. He is not one looking in from the outside regarding Medjugorje, but one who is close to the events—many times, right in the middle of the events about which he has written.

Originally writing to only a few individuals in 1987, readership has grown well into the millions in the United States and in over 130 foreign countries, who follow the spiritual insights and direction given through these writings.

When asked why he signs only as "a Friend of Medjugorje," he stated:

> *"I have never had an ambition or desire to write. I do so only because God has shown me, through prayer, that He desires this of me. So from the beginning, when I was writing to only a few people, I prayed to God and promised I would not sign anything; that the writings would have to carry themselves and not*

be built on a personality. I prayed that if it was God's desire for these writings to be inspired and known, then He could do it by His Will and grace and that my will be abandoned to it.

"The Father has made these writings known and continues to spread them to the ends of the earth. These were Our Lord's last words before ascending: ***'Be a witness to the ends of the earth.'*** *These writings give testimony to that desire of Our Lord, to be a witness with one's life. It is not important to be known. It is important to do God's Will."*

For those who require "ownership" of these writings by the 'witness' in seeing his name printed on this work in order to give it more credibility, we, Caritas of Birmingham and the Community of Caritas, state that we cannot reconcile the fact that these writings are producing hundreds of thousands of conversions, and will easily be into the millions, through God's grace. His writings are requested worldwide from every corner of the earth. His witness and testimony, therefore, will not take credit for a work that, by proof of the impact these writings have to lead hearts to conversion, has been Spirit–inspired, with numbers increasing yearly, sweeping as a wave across the ocean. Indeed, in this case, crossing every ocean of the earth. Our Lady gave this Witness a direct message, through the Medjugorje visionary, Marija, and part of what Our Lady said to him was to **"...witness not with words but through humility..."** (Oct. 6, 1986) It is for this reason that he wishes to remain simply, "A Friend of Medjugorje."

In order to silence the voice of this witness, darkness has continually spewed out slanders to prevent souls from reading his convicting and life-changing writings. For if these writings were not so, darkness would ignore them or even lead people to them. But Jesus promised persecution to all those who follow Him, and the same will be to those who follow His Mother. ***"If they persecuted me, they will also persecute you."*** John 15:20

As a witness in real time of Our Lady's time on earth, his witness and writings will continue to speak—voicing Our Lady's Way to hundreds of millions not yet born—in the centuries to come.

— Caritas of Birmingham

Open Your Eyes

One of the most pivotal books a Friend of Medjugorje has written to bring you and your loved ones towards a healthy family.

The Marriage Manua

SAVED HUNDREDS OF THOUSANDS OF MARRIAGES AROUND THE WORLD

How to Change Your Husband

Owner's Manual for the Family
By a Friend of Medjugorje

★Save & Renew Marriage
★Marriage Preparation
★Sermons for Your Pasto

See order form in the back of the book to order this book.

Searching for the Answer to Unconstitutional Government Lockdowns and Mob Violence

See order form in the back of the book to order this book.

DAVID ANSWER BY A FRIEND OF MEDJUGORJE

"...Not the President of the United States, not Congress, not the Supreme Court, not the mayor, but the local David holds the authority, and he is fast becoming the hero of the people. With the Spiritual, they are the answer to all the disorder..."

—From a Friend of Medjugorje in The David Answer

Make a Visit to:

Shortly after the founding of the Community of Caritas, a Friend of Medjugorje broke from the world's system and founded Our Lady of Victory's Little Schoolhouse in 1993. In this school, the vision and desire of a Friend of Medjugorje is to guide the Community and to teach and shape the children, just as Our Lady taught Jesus and His little friends. Our Lady, being the Mother of Christ, was the first Teacher of Jesus. Some of the saints saw in visions the Virgin teaching Her Son as a little Child, She who is Love. A Friend of Medjugorje has the students begin each day with the school prayer he wrote, which is addressed to Our Lady so that She would: ***"...Teach us and help us to understand that the most important lesson to learn is not from a book but how to love..."***

The Holy Spirit and Our Lady guide the choice of a different school theme every year, which has ranged from Kings and Queens, to Indians, to the Holy Land, to Pioneers, to God's Creation.

School is about learning and educating, but what, in particular should a child be learning in school? A Friend of Medjugorje raised his children to give them the life skills to, "get to Heaven and be able to put a roof over their heads." The 3 "Rs", reading, 'riting, and 'rithmetic, are taught in the little one-roomed schoolhouse. In addition, a large part of the teaching is done through apprenticeship. The students in Our Lady of Victory's Little Schoolhouse participate in meaningful work as part of their everyday life, side by side with the adults, in the agrarian work and the mission work.

The below picture is from the 2018–2019 School Year of Our Lady of Victory's Little Schoolhouse, the theme being "Washington's Dream & the Civil War." The school is filled with many graphics that help the children (and adults) grasp the principles of the theme for the entire school year. While the picture looks like a painting, the youth in the picture are real. The schoolhouse is open year round to visitors and school groups.

The Corona Vision

by a Friend of Medjugorje that is sweeping the world to bring clarity despite the political and media hype about the coronavirus, and what your future will be whether or not you want it.

$4.00 each book. As low as $1.00 each book for cases of 100.

"...The Corona Vision is a hope-filled future..."

—Dominic from Canada

THE CORONA VISION

by a Friend of Medjugorje

Order Form

	Item	Options	Amount
	**Has satan Pulled Another One on You?** Soft Cover Books BF124	*Please add shipping and handling* ❑ 1=$14.95 ❑ 3=$44.85 ($14.95 EA) ❑ 10=$149.50 ($14.95 EA) ❑ 25=$373.75 ($14.95 EA) *For quantities of 32 books or more see below*	$
	**I See Far** Soft Cover Books BF104	*Please add shipping and handling* ❑ 1=$7.00 ❑ 10=$40.00 ($4.00 EA)	$
	**How to Change Your Husband** Soft Cover Books BF103	*Please add shipping and handling* ❑ 1=$6.00 ❑ 10=$40.00 ($4.00 EA)	$
	**The David Answer** Soft Cover Books BF128	*Please add shipping and handling* ❑ 1=$7.00 ❑ 10=$40.00 ($4.00 EA)	$
	**The Corona Vision** Soft Cover Books BF126	*Please add shipping and handling* ❑ 1=$4.00 ❑ 10=$30 ($3.00 EA) ❑ 25=$50 ($2.00 EA) ❑ 50=$75 ($1.50 EA)	$
		Subtotal	$

Shipping & Handling

rder Sub-total	UPS SurePost (Standard)	UPS Ground
)-$10.00	$8.00	$15.00
10.01-$20.00	$10.50	$17.50
20.01-$50.00	$13.00	$20.00
50.01-$100.00	$20.00	$27.00
ver $100.00	20% of total	25% of total

For overnight delivery, call for pricing.
***International (Surface): Double above shipping Cost.
Call for faster International delivery.

$

Has satan Pulled Another One on You?
CASES OF 32 BOOKS For Economic Shipping

BF124–CASE Cases of 32 ($14.95 EA)
$478.40 + $45 S&H = $523.40

(UPS Shipping is included)

Cases	Qty.	Total
❑ 1	32	$523.40
❑ Other	____	($523.40 EA)

$

TOTAL: $

Ph: (Outside USA add 001)
05-672-2000 ext. 315 USA 24 hrs.
Fax: **205-672-9667 USA 24 hrs.**
) Mail: **Caritas of Birmingham**
Our Lady Queen of Peace Drive
rrett, AL 35147-9987 USA

Enclose in remittance envelope or call in your order and donation.
If you have any questions you may call 205-672-2000 and leave a message on ext. 315.
Or call during office hours 8:30 a.m.–5:00 p.m. Central Time
Monday–Friday and talk with a real person ☺
The Federal Tax Exempt I.D. # for Caritas of Birmingham is 63-0945243.

hip to: Name(s) (please print) ______________________ Birthday: __________
ddress ______________________________
ity ______________ State ______ Zip Code ____________
hone # ______________(if an international number, include all digits)
❑Payment Enclosed
redit Card type (check one) ❑ VISA ❑ MasterCard ❑ Discover
redit Card Number ☐☐☐☐ ☐☐☐☐ ☐☐☐☐ ☐☐☐☐ 3-Digit Code on Back: ☐☐☐
xpiration date: ☐☐-☐☐ e-mail: ______________________

Absolutely no names phone numbers addresses are sold or given away.

TO ORDER MORE COPIES OF

Has satan Pulled Another One On You?

Soft cover

CALL: Caritas of Birmingham

205-672-2000 ext. 315 twenty-four hours

or order on **mej.com** click on *"Shop Online"*

and click on *"Books by a Friend of Medjugorje"*

Call Caritas of Birmingham at
205-672-2000 for more information.